The French Army and Politics, 1870–1970

The French Army and Politics, 1870–1970

Alistair Horne

Peter Bedrick Books
New York

1/20/90

4

First American edition published by
Peter Bedrick Books
125 East 23 Street
New York, N.Y. 10010
Published by agreement with The Macmillan Press Ltd
London and Basingstoke

Library of Congress Cataloging in Publication Data

Horne, Alistair.
  The French Army and politics, 1870–1970.

  Bibliography: p.
  Includes index.
  1. France. Armée—Political activities. 2. France.
Armée—History—19th century. 3. France. Armée—
History—20th century. 4. France—Politics and govern-
ment—19th century. 5. France—Politics and government
—20th century. I. Title.
UA702.H67   1984   322'.5'0944   83–13453
ISBN 0–911745–15–7

Printed in Hong Kong
Distributed in the USA by Harper & Row
and in Canada by Book Center, Montreal

To Miles Norfolk

Contents

Contents

Author's Note and Acknowledgements

Since the Lees Knowles Lectureship in Military Science was founded just seventy years ago at Trinity, Cambridge, through the bounty of a former member of the College, it has invited annually an imposing galaxy of talent and distinction. On the list, Admirals, Field Marshals and Air Marshals jostle with Chichele Professors, eminent scientists and top civil servants. Among those of lower service rank figures that great Captain of military science, Basil Liddell Hart, while even the mere untitled embrace the names of Hilaire Belloc, Thomas Edward Lawrence and John Buchan (who, curiously, chose as his subject 'Oliver Cromwell as a Soldier'). In 1939 an unknown general called Sir A. P. Wavell gave his series of lectures (reputedly attended by only five students and a dog) on 'Generalship', which, read even now, comes across with the inspired simplicity of genius – unrecognised, as of that date, outside army circles. There is Lord Hankey (1944) on the 'Principles of Government Control in War', followed by Lord Tedder (1946) on 'Air Power in Modern Warfare', Fitzroy Maclean (1953) on 'Irregular Warfare', and – most recently – Field Marshal Lord Carver (1978) on 'The Apostles of Mobility'. On all of these topics, it would be hard to find greater expertise, as well as direct experience.

Thus when, very flatteringly, I was invited to give the Lees Knowles Lectures for 1982, I found it hard to think of any subject, not already covered, in which I could qualify among such illustrious precedents and of which I had special knowledge. In the past, students at Cambridge sitting an exam would sometimes be asked why they had chosen a certain question, and to answer 'it's the only one I know anything about' might gain points for honesty but was not a guaranteed path to a first. Nevertheless, such a consideration did, I suppose, influence my ultimate choice of 'The French Army and Politics, 1870–1970'. In the course of many years' researching for three books on Franco–German conflicts, followed by one on France's struggle in Algeria, the whole issue of the relationship between the French military and the politicians had come to fascinate me. In and out of each story the two partners weave like dancers, oscillating back and forth towards and away from one another. At times they are close to the point of total harmony (as in, though not always, the approach of war); at other times the army broods in self-imposed isolation, or is regarded with anxious mistrust by the politicians – with justification, or not.

Out of my researches, covering the century from 1870, I have consequently sought to distil the essence of this relationship; in particular I have tried to illuminate episodes where the military and the politicians have seemed to meddle, excessively or improperly, in each other's preserves, and to examine the results. Taken as a whole, I hope the lectures may act as something of a nexus in my past works, and also that they may provide the skeleton of something more substantial one day. Like the inept student who attempts to hide the sparseness of his knowledge by answering questions with widest possible spread, on writing them I swiftly realised, however, that I had probably erred in wanting to encompass a hundred years in four short lectures; approximately a generation an hour. Therefore, I plead to be forgiven if I seem over-selective, given to 'short-hand', or settling like a butterfly on certain specific episodes and issues.

I am obviously indebted to the Master and Senior Tutor of Trinity College, Cambridge, for their kind hospitality and the invitation which made this book possible. Further I am greatly beholden to the University of Western Ontario, Canada, who invited me to deliver three of the following lectures under their 'Joanne Goodman Lecture Series' for 1983, and to Mr Edwin Goodman personally for his warm hospitality. According to the terms of this generous memorial:

The JOANNE GOODMAN LECTURE SERIES has been established by Joanne's family and friends to perpetuate the memory of her blithe spirit, her quest for knowledge, and the rewarding years she spent at the University of Western Ontario.

I also wish to record, as another sad epitaph to a talented young woman, my own particular gratitude to Serena Booker, who helped me with all the additional research on the lectures, but was killed tragically before they were completed.

For specific information, help or advice given I am grateful to the following: His Excellency Evan Galbraith, US Ambassador in Paris, and Brigadier Patte and Colonel Grenier of the US Defence Attaché's staff in Paris; Contre-Amiral M. Mosnerot-Dupin and Colonel Bressey of the French Embassy in London; Dr Raymond Carr, Warden of St Antony's College, Oxford, Professor Michael Howard, MC, Regius Professor of History, and Professor Douglas Johnson of University College, London.

Among unpublished material used, I derived much benefit from the doctoral thesis kindly shown me by Martin Alexander, as well as from a *colloque* presented by him at the Sorbonne in May 1978: 'La faillite de la mécanisation dans les Armées Françaises et Britanniques entre 1935 et 1940 – une étude comparative'.

Publishers' Acknowledgements

The author and publishers wish to thank the following who have kindly given permission for the use of copyright material:

Cambridge University Press for an extract from *The March to the Marne* by D. Porch.

Harvard University Press for an extract from *Maxime Weygand and Civil–Military Relations in Modern France* by Philip C. F. Bankwitz.

Ohio State University Press for an extract from *The French Army in Politics 1945–1962* by John Steward Ambler.

Princeton University Press for an extract from *Parades and Politics at Vichy* by Robert O. Paxton. Copyright © 1966 by Princeton University Press.

University of California Press for an extract from *Generals and Politicians: Conflict between France's High Command, Parliament and Government 1914–18* by J. C. King.

Weidenfeld & Nicolson Ltd and George Braziller Inc. for an extract from *The French Army* by Paul-Marie de la Gorce.

Dr Theodore Zeldin for an extract from *France 1848–1945* published by Oxford University Press.

Publishers'
Acknowledgements

The author and publishers wish to thank the following who have kindly given permission for the use of copyright material:

Chronology

1851	Louis Napoleon's *coup d'état*.
1870	Franco–Prussian War: Louis Napoleon capitulates at Sedan and abdicates. Birth of Third Republic. Paris besieged.
1871	The Paris Commune established and destroyed.
1872–5	Three military laws lay basis for French military revival.
1877	*Seize Mai* constitutional crisis.
1886	General Georges Boulanger appointed Minister for War.
1889	Military law reduces conscription term from five to three years. End of post-1870 Army's 'Golden Age'.
1894	Dreyfus court-martialled.
1902	Emile Combes comes to power.
1905	Conscription reduced to two years.
1906	Dreyfus exonerated.
1911	German intervention at Agadir: Joffre appointed.
1913	Conscription restored to three years.
1914	The First World War begins; *Union Sacrée* founded.
1915	Joffre supreme.
1916	Verdun and the Somme.
1917	Joffre replaced by Nivelle; French Army mutinies; Nivelle replaced by Pétain.

1918	Winning combination of Clemenceau – Foch – Pétain leads France to victory.
1919	Clemenceau signs Versailles Treaty: Foch absents himself.
1923	Poincaré occupies Ruhr.
1930	Weygand replaces Pétain as Chief of the General Staff. De Gaulle publishes *Vers l'Armée de Métier*. Hitler rearms.
1935	Eighty-seven miles of Maginot Line completed.
1936	Gamelin replaces Weygand; France fails to react when Hitler re-occupies Rhineland.
1939	Nazi–Soviet Non-Aggression Pact. The Second World War begins.
1940	France defeated; Weygand refuses to continue war in North Africa. De Gaulle establishes Free French in London.
1941	British and Free French invade Syria.
1942	Allies land in North Africa; Germany moves into Unoccupied France.
1944	France liberated.
1945	End of the Second World War. Beginning of French War in Indo-China.
1954	Dien Bien Phu falls. End of Indo-China War. Beginning of Algerian War.
1956	Mollet sends conscripts to Algeria; Ben Bella hijacked; Anglo–French Suez operation.
1957	Massu wins 'Battle of Algiers'.
1958	Fourth Republic falls; Army takes over in Algiers; de Gaulle returns.
1959	De Gaulle offers Algerians 'self-determination'.
1960	Barricades Week revolt of Pieds Noirs. First French atom bomb exploded in Sahara. 'Manifesto of the 121' incites conscripts to desert.
1961	*Putsch de Généraux* in Algiers; OAS emerges.
1966	France leaves NATO.
1967	*Force de Frappe*; proclamation of *tous azimuts*.

1968   The May *événements*; de Gaulle flies to Germany
for Massu's support.

1970   Conscription reduced to twelve months.

1981   Mitterrand comes to power.

I

Flags in the Wind: The Commune to Dreyfus, 1870–1900

> The title [the Commune] was too imprecise to proclaim a programme, but, waving in the wind like a flag, it united the traditionalist souvenirs of some with the dreams of others and thus rallied French revolutionaries.
>
> Georges Laronze, *Histoire de la Commune de 1871; d'après des documents et des Souvenirs inédits*, 1928

De Gaulle, in *France et son Armée*, remarked in that sublimated manner of his, that the French were 'a people whose genius, whether in eclipse or in glory, has always found its faithful reflection in the mirror of its army'.[1] Any army – and perhaps more particularly the French – tends to reflect the political will which has shaped it, and thereby does provide the historian with a valuable microcosm of the society by which it is surrounded. As Theodore Zeldin observes in his imposing *France 1848–1945*, to the general historian the French Army also 'acts as a magnifying lens revealing aspects of national problems, and of personal tensions, more clearly than they can be seen in civil society'.[2]

1

On top of this, there is of course a certain value to be derived from the relevance to contemporary dilemmas of Western armies from some of the more violent episodes in the French experience. (If, for instance, the White House and the Pentagon had, between them, given closer study to the conflicts during the Algerian War between the French Military and Paris, might Vietnam have followed a different course?) But, if one has to seek a motive behind the title of this book, perhaps the most immediate might be to help explain why the French Army fought as it did, so very differently, on four various occasions:

- in 1870, with almost complete ineptitude
- in 1914, with heroic fortitude, final success, but colossal losses
- in 1940, with the most cataclysmic disaster
- in the post-1945 colonial wars of Indo-China and Algeria, where various blends of military competence found themselves in grave discord with the political will.

Let us try to identify some of the main themes, often inter-related and overlapping, that run through the hundred years from 1870 to 1970. First there is the precise function of the Army in the Republic, associated with the fears of some Republicans of what this might become. Seen from a telescope on the moon, the picture from as far back as 1815 right through to 1940 could appear to be a reassuringly tranquil one of civilian control over a compliant military establishment. In the words of Denis Brogan, the Army remained 'a faithful, even a docile servant of the state'.[3] But, close-up, what turbulence and eddies beneath the surface! And what constant, simultaneous struggles, during the first seventy years of our period, to maintain comparable efficiency with the natural enemy, Germany! It could perhaps be suggested that what did more damage to the French Army was not its disaffection or unreliability towards its Republican political masters, but their conceived apprehensions and mistrusts of the military's loyalty towards them. This book will reveal the truth of this, if any: I throw it out purely as a hypothesis – 'Discuss', as they say in the Tripos, 'with examples'.

Linked with this, there is the question of how much the French Army has been 'separate' and isolated from the Nation, or integrated within it. Different degrees at different times. 'The ideal constitution', declared General Trochu, who made himself unpopular under the Second Empire as a zealous military reformer, 'is that which creates an army whose instincts, beliefs, and habits make up a corporation distinct from the rest of the population.'[4] On the other hand over the years, many politicians – notably of the Left – have not found this notion very palatable.

Along this path one is led to the recurrent quandary that faced the political bosses: should they create an army that was politically reliable, or militarily effective? Were the two quite irreconcilable?[5] The bitter lessons of the Franco-Prussian War would tend to suggest that they were. And tangent to this quandary is the eternal politico-military argument of whether France should have an *armée de métier* (as espoused by Colonel de Gaulle in the 1930s), or a national conscript army with overtones harking back to the *levée en masse* of the Great Revolution. The argument has generally polarised between Left and Right; with the Left fearing that an *armée de métier* would be used to put down the workers, the Right seeing the conscript army as a political instrument with socialist, if not revolutionary, purposes. Closely associated with it, one must also consider the remarkable swings in the national attitude towards France's Army, the oscillations between wild-eyed patriotism and dour anti-militarism.

The obverse of this coin is, of course, how the Army felt about the Government and its prevailing policies at any given time. Outside the periods of euphoria and enormous effort, it was – in the words of de Gaulle – thrown into a 'melancholy'; which was a 'classically recurring situation'.[6] Nobody, of course, would be better placed than de Gaulle to apostrophise the vital contrasts between politician and soldier – though he wrote this many years before being himself called on to bridge the two:

> The one, who sees dimly from afar, judges realities to be complex and applies himself to grasp them by ruse and calculation; the other, who sees clearly but from close up, finds them to be simple and believes that one dominates them if only one is resolved to do so ... The soldier often considers the politician to be unreliable, inconsistent, eager for popularity.

How prophetic this would turn out to be in Algeria, with de Gaulle, the politician, damned as 'unreliable' and 'inconsistent' by *his* army.

Next one may come to the social composition of the Army's officer corps – were the aristocrats, bourgeois, or good Republican sons of 1889 in ascendance? What impact did this have on the minds of the politicians and their policies? And then, with special bearing on the first decades of the twentieth century, there was the red-hot issue (so strange to British or American experience) of Catholicism versus *Laicisme*.[7]

As a conjuror invites his audience to look carefully at the rabbit, so I must ask you to keep an eye on all this multitude of themes and issues. Finally, there is of course the overriding, key topic: the question of the army intervening in what are properly civil functions – and vice versa, the politicians interfering in strictly military matters.

Here one needs to attempt a difficult definition; what, in these contexts constitutes 'improper interference'? I have consulted the oracles – the Regius Professor, the Warden of St Antony's College, Oxford expert on modern Spain. The best answer I got is that it must all depend on what are the unwritten 'ground rules', or traditions applying, which may be different for each society. For instance, what might be construed a proper intervention by the army in nineteenth-century Spain would be considered improper in Aldershot; equally the army's involvement in the state in pre-1914 Germany was proper to Germany at the time, while it would not have been in Britain or the US. Today the 'lobbying' of the Pentagon for arms procurement in Washington, though it would seem highly improper in England, is all part of the 'American Way of Life'. In France in the 1930s, Weygand's flirtations with the extreme Right may have been imprudent, but not improper; however, his refusal in June 1940 to obey the Reynaud Government's order to continue the fight in North Africa was decidedly improper. The issue becomes distorted when an army claims, mystically, to be acting on behalf of Rousseau's 'General Will'; such as at a time when the democratic system has failed to fling up the true Will of the Nation. Such was the case in Algiers in May 1958;[8] while, of course, the Algerian War produces the most serious charges of 'impropriety' of the whole century. (It may be here worth recalling that Lord Wavell noted in the course of his Lees Knowles Lectures – in 1939 – that, although 'political generals' were anathema to British tradition, most of the best commanders – Cromwell, Marlborough, Wellington – all had political experience.)[9]

During the grim Miners' Strike winter of 1974, a foreign ambassador recently come from eight years in Paris asked me in all seriousness, 'Do you think the British Army would be reliable, if brought in?' I have to confess I laughed: the thought that they might prove otherwise would never have crossed my mind. But it would to a Frenchman of that period. Equally, American generals are amazed to be asked why none of them had resigned, let alone revolted, against LBJ's Vietnam policy – as did the French generals of Algiers against de Gaulle in April 1961.[10]

In one of the most majestic of all his wartime speeches,[11] Winston Churchill opened with the monumental statement: 'The Almighty in His infinite wisdom did not see fit to create Frenchmen in the image of Englishmen.' He then went on to explain, most movingly, the problems of political legitimacy which confronted a French soldier belonging to a state that had suffered so many convulsions.

Since the execution of Louis XVI in 1793, the French Army has been subject to the First Republic, the Directory, the Consulate, the First Empire, the First and Second Restorations, the 'Bourgeois Monarchy' of Louis-Philippe, and the Second Republic; while, just from the date where this book begins, we have the Second Empire, the Commune, the Third Republic, Hitler's Third Reich and Pétain's Vichy and de Gaulle's Free French Committee, the Fourth Republic, and finally de Gaulle's Fifth Republic. The French historian, Georges Laronze, once described the title of the Paris Commune of 1871 as being 'too imprecise to proclaim a programme, but, waving in the wind like a flag, it united the traditionalist souvenirs of some with the dreams of others and thus rallied French revolutionaries.'[12] Here, above, I have listed many more flags, all flapping about in the wind, uniting and disuniting Frenchmen. Each was to contribute new schisms in the Army, more confusion as to where loyalty was ultimately due, in a compound of experience shared by no other army in the world (outside, perhaps, Latin America). The theme 'the Army's been betrayed' runs close to the surface at various adverse moments in French history from 1870 to 1940; overlaid upon this came a non-stop series of humiliations leading in a straight line from 1940 to the Algerian War.

Now, of all these introductory remarks, I would most ardently beg you to bear in mind this one – the essential difference in the image of Frenchmen and Britons as decreed by the Almighty; and, through the course of this book be understanding of a prime and recurrent source of stresses, shocking and incomprehensible to the Anglo-Saxon mind, but one which we, in our history, have been mercifully spared.[13]

'In 1870', writes former Minister Alain Peyrefitte,[14] 'an impulse swept France into a confrontation with Germany which lasted for 75 years.' On 15 July of that year, Emperor Napoleon III, picking up Bismarck's adroitly cast gauntlet, launched France into one of the most disastrous wars in her history. There were fervid cries of '*à Berlin*' from the bellicose Paris mobs; but, instead, it was to Paris the Prussians came. 'France', said de Gaulle,[15] 'armed for a local war, was plunged into a war of nations.' One can summarise briefly the purely military causes – of which there are many – for the French Army's inadequacy. Too much misplaced self-confidence: it went to war with maps of Germany, but not of France. In a famous boast Marshal Leboeuf, the Minister of War, declared that the French troops departed 'ready to the last gaiter button' (which wags claimed was true, as there was not a gaiter in store anyway!). Despite his own endeavours of reform, Louis Napoleon's Army in 1870 went to war ill-equipped, badly led, trained and organised, and with inferior numbers.

On the other hand, von Moltke's Prussian Army was a superb instrument by any standard and would probably have beaten any other force of that period. Its steel, breech-loading cannon furnished by Herr Krupp were better than anything the French had; it had better generals and a general staff (which France lacked); it had a plan and it had battle experience – having defeated Austria in a lightning campaign at Sadowa four years previously. Most importantly, it had an advanced system of universal service and reserves, which meant that the German states could produce a force of 1 183 000 men within eighteen days of mobilisation. Nothing on this scale had ever been seen before. Through a first wartime usage of railways and telegraphs, Moltke was able to concentrate this potent mass at the decisive point far quicker than his adversary. Thus, in fact, the military odds against France were nearly as high as in 1940.[16]

But of more relevance to us is the politico-military background to all this; both in the disaster of 1870 itself, and in the much longer term. Nicknamed 'the Well-Meaning',[17] Louis Napoleon during the Second Empire had earnestly sought reform, social as well as military. But, in the classic case of an unlucky leader, everything had gone against him, and he had ended by only exacerbating Republican opposition. Particularly was this so in proletarian Paris, where the extreme Left was implacable – hating the moderate, bourgeois Republicans only little less than it did the Empire – with deadly consequences in 1871.[18]

As Michael Howard notes,[19] in the years following the Napoleonic Wars, most of the European powers shaped their forces as much for use in the suppression of insurrection at home as for fighting abroad. This was especially true of France; hence one more important reason for her inferiority *vis-à-vis* the Prussians in 1870. It also considerably affected both the role of the Army in the Nation, and how other Frenchmen regarded it. Still steeped in a residuum of the traditions of the Great Revolution, up to 1848 the Army was held to be, if anything, excessively liberal; with the lust for foreign adventures seeming to be a Republican prerogative.[20] It had compliantly obeyed the orders of its political masters; although, both in 1830 and 1848, its reluctance to fire on the revolutionaries had helped bring down those masters. Then, in 1852, it had been confronted with a choice of orders, and had chosen – by no means with total impropriety – to accept those of the (lawfully elected) President, Louis Napoleon, rather than of the (equally lawfully elected) Assembly, thereby enabling the coup through which Louis Napoleon established his Second Empire.[21]

Thus, after 1851, the Army had come to be recognised as the defender of the hierarchy; a situation which suited the bourgeoisie, but alienated the Republican foes of the Second Empire, who saw it now as an instrument of authoritarian repression. Indeed, under Louis Napoleon the Army was widely used – instead of the police – to break strikes as well as to head off revolution.[22] Conversely, the Army saw its own role as being one of upholding the existing regime, rather than attempting to alter or influence the political scene in any way; this despite the fact that some 30 per cent of the officer corps came from the nobility, and might therefore have been expected to support a restoration of the monarchy, while – as seen by the way they voted *Non* in Louis Napoleon's various plebiscites[23] – many others were at best lukewarm Bonapartists.

So, throughout the Second Empire, the Army cadres – worrying less about its legitimacy than they perhaps might have done – remained 'loyal' and 'reliable'. On the other hand, the divisive effect that the Army's role in the coup of 1851, and subsequently, had on the political scene bore the most baneful consequences for the state of France's military preparedness by 1870. Especially was this so when it came to opposing Louis Napoleon's military laws crucial to modernising universal service, and providing the reserves, such as Moltke was churning out on the other side of the Rhine. Universal service in France was a farce anyway, with a system of substitution whereby the moderately affluent bourgeois could, for a modest sum (of perhaps 1500 francs), purchase a substitute. The results were not all that dissimilar to those of college deferrals to the draft permitted in the US during the Vietnam War; the Army got the rag-tag-and-bobtail, the élite stayed out.[24] On top of this, as Eugene Weber reveals in his fascinating study, *Peasants into Frenchmen*, nineteenth-century rural France bore a far from united face and there were many areas where the Army was looked on as an occupation force; in Occitanie, to avoid conscription, men still knocked out their front teeth (without them, you couldn't tear open a musket cartridge), in Vaucluse even by 1873 things had still not changed much 'since the days when conscription had been resisted with pitchforks or by flight to the hills'.[25]

Meanwhile, in Paris the Right mistrusted a conscript army that smacked of the *levée en masse* for obvious political reasons, and clamoured for a strong professional *armée de métier*, not just as a bastion against the menace abroad, but at home too. The Left saw this, saw the muskets pointing at them, and reacted accordingly. Thiers, the historian who described himself as 'a monarchist who practices republicanism',[26] had studied the lessons of the First Empire and always believed in the superiority of professional armies. But most Republicans agree with his colleague, Jules Simon, who declared during the debate on the Draft Law of 1867, just three years before war began, 'We want an army of citizens which would be invincible on its home soil, but incapable of carrying a war abroad.'[27] Battling the creation of a *Garde Mobile*, the territorials that might have provided the answer to the Prussian reservists, Simon accused the Government's intent of being 'the organisation of war; ours, exceptionally defensive, is the organisation of peace'.[28] In vain did Prévost Paradol criticise the left-wing opponents of 'the strong army', on the grounds that 'defensive' war demands as skilful soldiers as 'offensive' war. (In 1870, newly appointed Ambassador to Washington, Prévost-Paradol, warned his countrymen, 'you will not go to Germany, you will be crushed in France. Believe me, I know the Prussians.' Then he committed suicide.)[29] The further to the Left in the political spectrum, the more fervent was the antimilitarism. Angrily the reforming General Trochu (an Orleanist who was certainly, as events proved, no devotee of the Emperor) apostrophised the Left as 'the eternal enemies of order'.[30]

So the internal battle lines were drawn up for 1870,

while the same basic arguments, on both sides, would be echoed through the French Assembly for the next seventy years – with equal damage. When Louis Napoleon's new military law finally emerged in 1868, sharply whittled down by opposition, it showed little advance on the old. As France went to war, the *Garde Mobile* was still not much more than an idea.[31]

On 1 September 1870, after just six weeks of *blitzkrieg*-like victories, Moltke cornered Louis Napoleon at the head of his army at Sedan the scene of a second cataclysmic French defeat in 1940. Three days after his humiliation a revolt in Paris deposed the captured Emperor and declared a Republic. Against now hopeless odds the new Government – under General Trochu – decided to continue the war. Contrary to all expectations, Paris, besieged and reduced to eating cats, dogs and rats, held out bravely for over four months while Gambetta raised new armies in the provinces.[32]

During the course of the Siege of Paris, Marshal Bazaine, invested at Metz with his army and with considerably slimmer prospects than those of the Paris garrison, surrendered after resisting for two months. Bazaine's capitulation undoubtedly reduced the ability of the capital to hold out, and – though once immensely popular as a fearless soldier risen from the ranks – he became the war's scapegoat and was sentenced to death for treason, although this was later commuted to life imprisonment. Militarily, his faults were more of incompetence than treason; but what most interests us here is that Bazaine represents the *sole* case, up to 1940, of a French senior officer taking a military decision (against his orders) out of political motivation. His dilemma was one of legitimacy; maintaining a perhaps misplaced loyalty toward the deposed Emperor, while he detested the new Republican Government and rejected its authority. 'I had no government', he declared at his trial; 'I was, so to speak, my own government.'[33]

11

In substitution for the missing *Gardes Mobiles* in Paris, Trochu created a locally recruited National Guard. He ignored Machiavelli's elementary warning: 'He who commands the defence of a town will shun arming the citizens.'[34] Virtually useless as soldiers, and electing their own officers from the most articulate left-wing revolutionaries, the National Guard soon proved to be a political time bomb. One key factor behind the long-protracted endurance of besieged Paris was the emergence to the far left of Trochu's new Republican Government of ginger groups composed of ardent revolutionaries. A strange metamorphosis had taken place; the former anti-militarists, opponents of the 'strong' national army had now become super-hawks who – rediscovering themselves to be the true heirs to the *levée en masse* of the Great Revolution – demanded that the war be fought to the bitter end. They had their reasons. They feared that the moderate bourgeois Republicans – whom they regarded as having cheated them out of the spoils of three past revolutions, 1789, 1830 and 1848 – would now do a deal with the Prussians, ending the war and restoring the hated *status quo ante*. Two serious revolts inside the capital persuaded Trochu's moderates that to fight on against the Prussians was the lesser of two evils.

This in fact only postponed the inevitable. On 27 January 1871 an armistice was signed. Infuriated by this capitulation, followed by elections which returned an even more conservative Republican government, the Paris 'Reds' of the National Guard rose up in March and seized an armoury of cannon from the bemused regular army. Thiers, the new provisional President, realising his impotence and the imminent danger of civil war, withdrew the government and the army to Versailles. The 'Reds', or *fédérés*, were left in sole charge of Paris and promptly proclaimed a 'Commune' – which was to last seventy-two days. A highly complex amalgam, but in effect a rival government with strong Jacobin undertones from the Great Revolution, the Commune – despite its name – had little or nothing to do with Communism, although it was greatly to influence both Marx and Lenin, as well as subsequent generations of the French Left.

Under Bismarck's armistice terms the French regular army had been much reduced, and – had the Communards marched at once on Versailles – they could probably have seized Thiers's Government and made themselves masters of France. But they missed the bus, and from April to May the Second Siege of Paris took place; this time conducted by French government troops against the Parisian Communards. At the end of May Paris was invaded and the Commune put down in an appalling bloodbath, with the estimated slaughter of over 20 000 Communards.[35]

Back in March, when the regular troops had fraternised with the *fédérés* making off with their guns, the army's reliability appeared extremely shaky. One soldier was recorded as saying, 'If they make me march against the Parisians, I shall march .. but in no case will I fire against them.'[36] From then on Thiers and the army generals had to move with great caution so as not to demand too much of the Army: yet even up to the middle of the fighting its value remained questionable.[37] By the end of May, however, a remarkable transformation had occurred, with the regulars showing themselves prepared to crush their kinsmen with the utmost ferocity. Why the change of heart? In his book, *The War Against Paris*, Dr Robert Tombs offers three useful explanations: first of all the Army saw itself as representing order against the mounting anarchy of the Commune. Predominantly bourgeois, the officers feared and hated the Communards' seizure or destruction of private property, culminating in the wilful conflagration of large parts of Paris during the final *semaine sanglante*. Secondly, it represented the nation against faction. Thirdly, it held itself to be the champion of liberty against tyranny.[38]

On the crushing of the Commune, Thiers boasted, 'We have got rid of Socialism.'[39] He was, of course, totally wrong; history was to prove that the death of the Commune, with all the mythology it left behind fanned by Marx, was far more important than its life. A deep trench had been dug between the bourgeoisie and the masses, between the professional army and the Left, which would stretch on into the far distance, suddenly yawning open to bedevil at various crucial moments relations between the military and he political.[40] One immediate legacy of the nightmare of the Franco-Prussian War and the Commune was to persuade France's political leaders that henceforth the Army would have to be treated with the utmost tender loving care. 'The army had been brought into politics by the civil war', Dr Tombs writes of its aftermath:

> The extreme Right saw it as a bulwark of society . . . but even with MacMahon as President, the army made no move to stem the tide of Left-wing advance, however much its officers would have liked to try. The lesson of March 18 seems to have been learnt: that the cohesion of the army itself was put at risk by involvement in internal disputes . . . The army had won a military victory in 1871, but had been forced to realise the limits of military victory.[41]

This was to apply for many years to come.

After the dual catastrophe of 1870–1 France made a miraculously rapid recovery, despite the crippling reparations levied by Bismarck. Central to it was the reinvigoration of the Army, symbol of France resurrected. 'Everything was rotten in France', Thiers had told officers during the war, 'only the army remained clean and honourable.'[42] Hence what better starting point for a spiritual spring cleaning than the Army? Hand in hand with a wave of piety in the nation, a new mood of dedication ran through the whole army, determined to expunge the blots on its reputation; while the loss of Alsace-Lorraine gave it a new sense of purpose, *la Revanche*. In marked contrast to the Second Empire when

MacMahon had threatened 'I shall remove from the promotion list any officer whose name I read on the cover of a book', young officers like Foch, Pétain and Joffre began to make penetrating studies of the 1870 campaign. The ways of the conqueror, his discipline and organisation, were emulated without shame.[43] A brief Golden Age opened (and lasted some twenty years), in which the nation lent its almost whole-hearted support to military revival. Whereas in the provinces there had been anti-war riots in 1870, with – so Eugene Weber tells us – even cries of 'Long Live Prussia!', after 1871 Alsace-Lorraine began to ring the changes; so that by 1880 there was persuasive evidence that the Army was 'no longer "theirs" but "ours".'[44]

The national pulse was reflected in three military laws of 1872, 1873 and 1875 whereby the foundations were laid upon which the French Army of 1914 was to be built. They established universal military service, putting an end to the evils of substitution, and providing the cadre of reserves that France had lacked in 1870.[45] This meant, in effect, that – for the time being at least – politicians and soldiers alike had learned one lesson from 1870. In the words of Michael Howard, 'The small, introvert professional army, more conscious of its social than its professional status, was no longer an effective form of military organisation.'[46] Though Thiers remained as wedded as before to the superiority of the *armée de métier*, the Right as a whole had completely broken with its earlier philosophy and accepted the principle of compulsory military service; while with surprising equanimity the Left, in 1872, accepted the obvious social inequality of the five years service. In 1880, Gambetta's Amnesty Bill even went some way to heal the wounds left by the Commune. The post-1871 Army was well-nicknamed the 'Ark of the Covenant', in that it was unassailable and sheltered from the violent political quarrels which had buffeted the Third Republic on its creation.

Of this honeymoon period, de Gaulle remarks accurately, 'Though his pay is meagre, the officer is compensated by the exceptional prestige he enjoys.'[47] Now chic and 'respectable', the Army drew to it larger numbers than heretofore of the conservative, Catholic aristocracy and bourgeoisie. In his novel *L'Emigré*, Paul Bourget says, through the mouth of Lieutenant de Claviers-Granchamps:

> I had no choice ... Every career was barred to the future Marquis de Claviers-Granchamps. Yes, barred. Foreign affairs? Barred. My father, at least, would have been accepted by the Empire. Today we are no longer desired. The Council of State? Barred. The Administration? Barred. Can you see a noble acting as Prefect of a Department? ... The Army alone was left me.

A young officer, whose name will appear frequently later on in the book, Maxime Weygand, claims that when he was contemplating a military career in 1885, 'They told me... that the Army was the thing for nobles without a fortune.'[48] On the other hand, there were staunch Imperial generals from pre-1870, who – like the dashing General Gallifet, the fierce slayer of Communards – became disenchanted with the incompetence of the Second Empire and were transformed into loyal and staid Republicans. Conservative though many of its officers might be, in its outward trappings the new Army was safely Republican, and largely apolitical. Yet – more than its conservative components – this very apoliticalism tended to make it stand further apart from the rest of the nation, a condition accentuated as the century approached its close, and which in itself continued to attract the mistrust of Republican politicians as we shall see later.

It is thus not by chance that perhaps the most effective Minister of the young Third Republic was its first non-military incumbent, Charles Freycinet, the brilliant organiser of the Armies of the Provinces in 1870. Misleadingly nicknamed 'the little white mouse', Freycinet believed it was leaders more than numbers that had brought Prussia victory. He thus dedicated himself to equipping the Conseil Supérieur de la Guerre (CSG) with the kind of teeth which distinguished the General Staff apparatus of the natural enemy, Germany, and to insulate the CSG from the kind of ministerial instability which, in France, had produced nineteen governments and sixteen War Ministers between 1870 and 1888, when Freycinet came to office. Now, only a trusted Republican politician like Freycinet could have pushed through the reforms required to strengthen the CSG or to create the key post of Chief of the Army General Staff, as was done in May 1890.[49]

In a secret report prepared for Gambetta in 1876–8, and only recently uncovered, the authors claimed that 70 per cent of army officers listed were 'conservatives', 'reactionaries', 'Bonapartists', or 'Royalists'. If this is what the Republican leaders were being told at the time, it is not unreasonable for subsequent historians perhaps to have exaggerated the importance of conservative influences in the post-1870 French Army. To go back to what I suggested earlier, what seems to be much more significant is what the Republican politicians thought and feared about all this.

Of course there were genuine frights and flutters. There was the *seize mai* crisis of 1877, when the young Republic faced the constitutional issue of whether the President (who unfortunately happened to be a soldier, Marshal MacMahon) could dismiss a Government regardless of its parliamentary majority. Fears of an army coup ran through the Assembly; but in fact the Army remained loyally intact, and the crisis was resolved partly through the blinkered legalism of MacMahon. Meanwhile, Republican ascendancy during this period was also clearly demonstrated by the summary sacking of General Ducrot, sturdy hero of the Siege of Paris, five other corps commanders, and the C-in-C of the Mediterranean fleet, for making improper political noises. All this was accepted by the Army with barely a murmur.[50]

More flamboyant, though possibly less serious, was the extraordinary nine days' wonder of General Boulanger. Appointed in 1886, Boulanger was a better War Minister than he has generally been credited; he was also a self-declared devout Republican – though his subsequent actions showed that, when it came to personal ambition, he might not be beyond a raid on the Tabernacle. His waving the flag of *revanche*, as well as his swashbuckling personal allure, made a dramatic appeal to that irrational longing in the French character for the 'man on the white horse'. On the streets, inflammatory songs were heard that seemed painfully evocative of the summer of 1870:

> *Regardez-le là-bas! Il nous sourit et passe*
> *Il vient de délivrer la Lorraine et l'Alsace.*

In Berlin, Bismarck's finger crooked nervously round the trigger; but, fortunately for France, Boulanger lost his nerve – followed by his credibility. His suicide on the grave of his mistress was to provoke Clemenceau's brutal epitaph, about his dying 'as he had lived, like a subaltern'. Again, what was truly important in this episode was the Army's total disinclination to follow whatever lead Boulanger might have offered.[51]

In August 1876, a Bonapartist deputy had challenged the primacy of Republican civilian authority when he declared, 'The Army is above existing institutions', but was promptly shot down by the President of the Chamber, Jules Grévy. 'Nothing', pronounced Grévy, 'is above institutions, nothing is above the law of the nation, and nothing is more revolutionary ... more factious, than putting the military forces above the law.' This declaration was to remain *the* article of faith of military-political relations in France throughout most of the life of the Third

Republic, certainly through the rest of the century, and it was widely accepted by the Army. Yet the Boulanger interlude, absurd though it was, in another sense marked an important watershed in these relations. You cannot sustain military enthusiasm indefinitely – especially in a nation as volatile and as plagued by *l'ennui* as France. *La Revanche* seemed more remote and unattainable than ever; there were plums to be won in colonies abroad, appealing distractions to mitigate the pain of the amputated territories; and *la vie douce* had become wonderfully good in France itself. Towards the end of the century, France was beginning to grow weary of her army and its Minotaur-like demands on the nation's youth – as well as its riches. In 1889 General Gallifet, then War Minister, lost a long struggle to maintain the term of national service, with the law of that year reducing it from five to three years. Although this still procured for the Army some 250 000 conscripts each year, it heralded the end of the Golden Age that had endured since 1871, and the beginning of another long tug-o'-war between the military and the politicians.[52]

Now, amid increasing new strains of anti-militarism, the century closes with the long, sombre shadow of Dreyfus falling across the French Army's path of revival on its way to the terrible test of 1914.

II

The Union Sacrée, 1900–18

The ancient Romans put up a statue to the general who saved them in one of Rome's darkest hours, with this inscription: 'Because he did not despair of the Republic.'

General Sir Archibald Wavell,
'The Soldier and the Statesman'
Lees Knowles Lecture, 1939

There are times in the course of human history when – like the Gadarene Swine, or the lemmings swimming out to sea – societies suddenly behave with total, self-destructive irrationality, against all predictable dictates of reason. One may think of the Albigensian Crusade, the Witches of Salem, the Terror of 1793, the Soviet purges of the 1930s – and nearer our day perhaps Suez, the Chinese Cultural Revolution and even Watergate. But, as one stands back further in time from the Dreyfus Case, it seems to sit on a special pinnacle of collective madness all on its own; and, when one examines the passions it unleashed, one becomes rather less surprised that the greatest mass madness of all, 1914, lay only a few years ahead.

The whole sordid story is so well known that there is

scarcely need to rehearse it in detail all over again: the damning *bordereau* of French military secrets, allegedly bearing the handwriting of Dreyfus, the Jewish captain; the court martial of 1894, followed by the life sentence on Devil's Island; the discovery of Esterhazy's guilt, and the Ministry of War's attempt to hush it all up; Zola's *J'Accuse* and the powerful public emotions whipped up for a retrial; the suicide of Colonel Henry, Dreyfus's accuser, the forger and dubious protector of the Army's honour; the retrial of 1899, the pardon and finally the reversal of the sentence in 1906. These were twelve years that tore French society apart in the most appalling way, re-opening all the cicatrices that had been healing since 1871, and exposing some new ones – such as the gangrenous sore of anti-semitism. But what we must confine ourselves to here is to what the Dreyfus Case did to the French Army, in its relations with the political.

With extraordinary swiftness 'The Affair' escalated far beyond the simple issue of the guilt or innocence of one man. At this range, it is difficult to appreciate the bitterness generated, where even the highest in the land became involved. (At one point the newly elected pro-Dreyfus President, Loubet, had his top hat cleft at the race course by the cane of an anti-Dreyfus baron.) It was as if some Pandora's box full of all the suppressed and most violent prejudices of the past century had suddenly been opened. Across the nation attitudes polarised and hardened, with the Dreyfusards seen as Republican and progressive, standing for justice and individual liberty and supported by the intelligentsia; on the other hand, the Army – from whose closed ranks the scandal had sprung – partly Monarchist and largely Catholic, dedicated to hierarchical order, tradition and obedience. As the crisis deepened, and the Army closed its ranks from external attack, so it seemed to stand further and further apart from the rest of the nation. Despite appearances, however, the Army was not entirely monolithic over Dreyfus. If there was Major

Henry, the former NCO of peasant stock whose blind loyalty to his superiors and to army discipline was to lead him to unscrupulous dishonesty and forgery, there was also Colonel Picquart, whose unequivocal passion for justice brought him into breach with the loyalties and beliefs of his whole life – and proved most inconvenient to those of the army command who wanted The Affair to be hushed up and forgotten.[1]

The point came when the Army had reason to feel its whole being was under attack from its Republican foes, and there was talk of a right-wing military coup. At the funeral of President Félix Faure, who died in his office supposedly in a dialogue – unsuitable to his age – with a lusty redhead, Paul Deroulède, the fiery *revanchist* founder of the *Ligue des Patriotes*, grabbed the bridle of an unknown general, crying, 'Follow us, General, for the sake of France!' But the general refused to follow – as did the rest of the Army throughout the Affair. There were officers who were guilty of bad faith, and disobedience; but, as an entity, the Army, once again, did nothing more disloyal than to grumble.[2] Its determination, however, to save the face of the General Staff, regardless of justice for a Jewish captain, was to do it incalculable damage. Relations with Republican politicians reached the lowest ebb since 1871, with the Radicals – their power much enhanced by 'The Affair' – particularly asking the question: Can an authoritarian and introverted army, with paramount interest in the sheltering of its own kin, co-exist side by side with a democratic regime? Their conclusions gave the politicians the opportunity to claw back much of the ground which had been handed the Army during the Golden Age of military resuscitation. The authority of the Minister of War, and through him, parliament, was strengthened – at the cost of the newly constituted, and estimable, command structure, for which that good Republican, Freycinet, had fought so hard. In *M. Bergeret*, written at the height of The Affair, Anatole France has a character speak of the Army as representing 'all that is left of our glorious past. It consoles us for the present and gives us hope of the future.' But this was hardly a majority view at the time. Worst of all, the Army had now ceased to be *the* institution that was considered to be above all faction.[3]

Following the retrial of Dreyfus, General Gallifet, then Minister of War, gave out a famous order to the Army: 'The Army belongs to no party, it belongs to France ... the incident is closed.' But the politicians jeered: 'Platoon! Attention! On my command, by the left flank, forget!'[4]

It would be a very long time before the incident could be truly considered closed. On its heels, and closely linked with it, as a kind of reaction, there occurred an interlude which, to English minds, smacked of Henry VIII in the twentieth century. In 1902, Emiles Combes, an anti-clerical Radical possessed of all the prejudices of a small-town provincial, came to power with a mandate to 'republicanise' the administration, the Church and the Army. Strongly supported by Radicals and Socialists, he was determined to complete the separation of Church and State and swiftly legislated the dissolution of all 'unauthorised' religious orders – some of which had admittedly intervened in a most rashly improper fashion during The Affair.[5] Schools were closed, even religious processions were stopped, and, in the expropriations of nunneries and monasteries, wanton pillaging occurred.

Then the Army was finally called in to effect the expropriations, thereby confronting its practising Catholics with a grave issue of conscience, parallel to that experienced by the British Army over the Curragh Mutiny a few years later. One French lieutenant-colonel, when he enquired what his regimental commander was going to do, was told: 'I have flu'; whereupon, in a rage transcending rank, he seized his superior fiercely, shouting, 'I suppose when the war comes you will have flu too!' National divisions created by The Affair now began to spread through the Army. But there was worse to come. As his last act as War Minister, Gallifet, in whom The Affair had left no good opinion of the Army leaders, declared the army promotion committees to be merely consultative, and passed the ultimate responsibility for promotion to the War Minister.[6]

His successor, General André, was a distinguished scientist and gunner who introduced the heavy 155 mm cannon, which may well have saved France in the desperate days after 1914. His chief claim to the post, however, was a reputation as the only *général de division* who was a 'safe' Republican, and as dedicated an anti-clerical as Premier Combes, and he deplorably abused the power passed on to him by Gallifet. 'Promotion', he declared, 'is in the hands of Parliament.' His first aim was to single out from the 'silent and anonymous' ranks of the officer corps those who could be relied upon 'because of their Republican sentiments'. This signified something never before attempted by a War Minister of the Third Republic; a fundamental purge of the political, and religious, ideals of the officers of the French Army. 'I will remain at my post, and I will never be removed from the Ministry except as a corpse,' promised André. But it looked more likely that the corpse might be that of the French Army.[7]

André attacked his goal by setting officers to spy on each other; and – foolishly – he employed the Grand Orient Lodge of Freemasons as an intelligence service to establish dossiers, or *fiches*, on their political and religious persuasions. The *affaire des fiches* was exposed, and both André and the Combes Government fell, but by this time the damage was done – and it was colossal. Officers began to concentrate their energies on currying political favour; visiting a garrison in 1900, André was gratified to note how officers who had previously denounced him in unprintable language, now rushed to shake his hand:

I then understood the devotion which a regime making such

dreams possible can inspire in its favourites pulled from obscurity.

A devastating admission. Logistically, it was easier for slouches on the staff in Paris than for talented regimental officers in the Provinces to catch the Minister's eye, and become 'favourites'. Inevitably standards slumped; sluggish bureaucracy thrived. Even by 1910, 34.5 per cent of captains in the infantry department of the War Ministry were promoted major, compared to 1.5 per cent from line regiments; while 31.9 per cent of all officers joining the Pay Corps became brigadiers and generals, compared with 9.6 per cent for combat arms. Smart officers flocked to join the administrative branches. Emile Driant, a brilliant Chasseur officer, deputy and author of many imaginative books, who was to die in command of one of the most inspired actions at Verdun in 1916, was passed over for promotion five successive years after 1900; his sin, to have been ADC to General Boulanger and marry the boss's daughter. How often an officer attended church also assumed an absurd degree of priority over merit, with the *fiches* collected by General André bearing such comments as 'Goes to mass ... His brother is a Jesuit.' Promotion lagged for officers like Foch, whose brother was a Jesuit, and de Castelnau, who was accompanied to the war by his own private chaplain and whose Catholicism – it was generally believed – deprived him of the Marshal's baton he merited. As late as 1917, the newly appointed and respectable Protestant C-in-C, Nivelle, could fly into a rage on discovering that his HQ had once been a Catholic priests' seminary; and it was no coincidence that, in 1911, the office of the new Chief of the General Staff would fall to a general who ostentatiously ate meat on Good Friday.

To return to my attempt in the first chapter to define what constitutes 'improper interference', I would rate General André's political interference in army promotions as one good example of *high* impropriety; and an impropriety that was exceeded only by the direness of its consequences for the French Army.[8]

Dreyfus, Combes and André were accompanied by the most intense bout of anti-militarism that France had experienced since 1870. Already in 1887 Abel Hermant's novel, *Le Cavalier Miserey*, had appeared, attacking corruption and poor conditions in the Army, and by the turn of the century writing an anti-militarist novel had almost become the accepted way for a young author to make his mark. Dreyfus helped convert Anatole France to socialism, and as memories of Alsace-Lorraine receded, so anti-militarism grew more fashionable – in bourgeois circles as well as among the left intelligentsia. 'Personally, I would not give the little finger of my left hand in exchange for these forgotten lands,' wrote Rémy de Gourmond in the *Mercure de France* in 1891.[9]

A more dramatic source of unpopularity was the Army's involvement in strike-breaking. In 1906, the CGT Congress proclaimed: 'Anti-militarist and anti-patriotic propaganda must become ever more intense and more audacious. In every strike the Army is for the employers.'[10] In France, the first decade of the new century saw a great increase in working-class unrest, and in 1906 even the arch-Radical and anti-militarist, Clemenceau, when Minister of the Interior, found himself forced to use troops against striking miners. That same year, at the peak of Franco-German tension, the CGT organ *La Voix du Peuple* (in a manner somewhat comparable to the famous Oxford Union motion of the 1930s) called on French workers 'to refuse to take up arms in the event of war with Germany'. The rank and file of the Army was far from happy with their role as strike-breakers. During the 1907 crisis in the wine industry, troops of the 100th Infantry Regiment sent to quell riots in Béziers, in the south-west, actually mutinied in sympathy with the populace. When rumours reached other parts of France that the troops had fired on the crowd, conscripts from the region told their officers, 'We want to go to Béziers to defend our parents who are being murdered.'[11]

What effect did all this have on the capability of the French Army? In 1905, a new Act had already cut national service to two years, reducing the size of the Army from 615 000 to 504 000 men. Two years later 36 per cent of territorials due for service failed to report. Between 1907 and 1909 the numbers of desertions multiplied from 5000 to 17 000; while between 1906 and 1911 the number of disciplinary courts martial doubled. The social and economic plight of officers had become grave; pay compared poorly with that of their German counterparts, and (in 1913) a French Major-General would receive one-third the pension which his British opposite number could anticipate. An officer might remain a lieutenant for twelve to fifteen years, a captain for another fifteen to twenty. As one captain wrote in an Army magazine in 1905,

> Ten or twenty years ago the officer with his mind set on marriage attired himself in dress uniform and white gloves in order to seek out his prospective father-in-law. Today he scarcely dares confess that he is an officer.

It is hardly surprising that, between 1900 and 1911, officer candidates fell from 1895 to 871; whereas St Cyr in 1890 was accepting only one in five of applicants, by 1913 the choice had fallen to one in two. At the same time, as a result of General André's ravages of the General Staff, the Army found itself virtually a body without a head.[12]

All this reflected the nadir of prestige to which the Army had sunk, which in turn reflected the distrust for the Army Establishment generated since Dreyfus. This distrust was shared by politicians of almost all hues, but was – naturally enough – at its most violent on the Left, among the Socialists. In 1908, the year after the Béziers troubles, the CGT at its congress in Marseilles went so far as to vote, 'The workers will reply to a declaration of war with the declaration of a revolutionary general strike.' It was indicative of how dangerously wide the gulf between the Army and the Left had once again become; a gulf that would go on plaguing French defence policy not only up to 1914, but on into the post-1918 era.

Happily for France, however, the Socialists at this time threw up one of their truly great leaders, the fearless Jean-Léon Jaurès. Jaurès was unique, both in his party and the whole contemporary political scene, in being an independent-minded and innovative military thinker. Though true to his background in opposing the *armée de métier*, wanting in its place something akin to the Swiss citizens' militia, he was a true patriot who saw the urgent need for France to prepare, once again, to defend herself, An anti-militarist, but not anti-army, Jaurès with his calm, sound counsel did much to restore French unity on the eve of war; even though, at that critical moment, he himself was to be struck down by a Nationalist fanatic.[13]

This grave decline in the French Army over the first decade of the century bears some comparison to the Tukhachevsky purges of the Soviet Army in the 1930s, from which it had certainly not recovered by June 1941, and – alas for Europe – both occurred at a time when the natural enemy, Germany, had reached a peak of strength and aggressiveness. Having duly noted all that was passing in France, the Kaiser was encouraged to commit that deadly sin of great leaders; speculation. He began by butting into France's protectorate, Morocco, with little idea of where it would all end. After the Agadir crisis of 1911, a sharp accentuation of military fervour swept both Germany and France. The nation found itself deeply alarmed at the new bellicosity across the Rhine; coupled with this went the sudden realisation of how, dramatically, over the two generations since 1870, the population of Germany had risen in relation to France's – and thence her capacity to field an army of vast reserves. At the same time, the military value – in the event of war – of France's two new Allies, Russia and Britain, was disquietingly hard to assess. Conceivably the depth of anti-militarism of the past decade in France had been misgauged; in any event it now reversed itself with astonishing speed, with the writings of the arch-patriot Maurice Barrès (who took it upon himself to teach French youth how to die beautifully) suddenly enjoying an enormous vogue. When 1914 came even the septuagenarian anti-militarist, Anatole France, promptly tried to join the colours.

So from 1911 onwards, grimly in tune with the mood seizing the rest of Europe, France plunged herself wholeheartedly into a patriotic *Réveil National*. It was, to quote the words of the American historian David B. Ralston, 'one of those nebulous but nevertheless real phenomena in history which can be neither wholly explained not discounted'.[14]

In 1913, the law restoring military service from two to three years was passed with utmost speed, amid patriotic scenes strongly tinged with chauvinism, and was greeted with remarkable good humour by the nation at large. This was all very different from the wrangling and bitterness that had surrounded the 1905 Act, the damage of which was now to a large extent reversed.[15]

In an interesting recent study, *The March to the Marne*, Douglas Porch argues the importance of the Colonial Army in France's *Réveil National* of pre-1914, and this might be the place to make a brief allusion to it. By 1914, France (encouraged by Bismarck, who had cynically hoped imperial expansion would distract her from the loss of Alsace-Lorraine) ruled over the world's second greatest colonial empire, with fifty million inhabitants. Contrary to Bismarck's calculations, it made France a great deal richer and more powerful when war finally came, as well as providing her with an additional 500 000 excellent troops for use both on the Western Front and in the Near East. Apart from this, as Porch rightly points out, officers of the Colonial Army (like Galliéni, the saviour of Paris in

1914; Mangin the hero of Villers-Cotterets in 1918, and to an extent even Joffre himself) provided a rejuvenating 'shaft of light' during the dark years of civil-military relations, when 'soldiers who were distrusted, spied upon and humiliated in France were pampered, promoted and decorated abroad'. The future Marshal Lyautey, France's greatest paladin of Empire, wrote home ecstatically in 1894:

> What careers there are to be established and led here! Here there is not one of these little lieutenants ... who does not develop more initiative, will, endurance and personality in six months than does an officer in France in his entire career.

Away from the stultifying influences of Paris and War Ministers like General André, colonial officers were encouraged to show independence of mind, and action. As early as the 1840s, in North Africa the *Bureaux Arabes* had converted many officers into civil administrators with extensive local powers, and the name of the game was that the Colonial Army officers were primarily administrators, and good ones, rather than combat soldiers.

All this was to play a significant role in the immediate drama of 1914–18; and again in the post-war world after 1918, but, of course, even more so after 1945.[16]

When war came, in August 1914, it was France's good fortune that the civil-military foundations, on which the structure of the new post-1871 Army had been built, proved to be still fundamentally sound; despite the effect of the intervening years of unpopularity and neglect and of the even longer years of no combat experience. In marked contrast to 1870, mobilisation ran with superb smoothness. Nearly two million men were brought into position by 4278 trains, and of all the trains set in motion only nineteen ran late. Much of the credit for this achievement must go to Joffre, the new C-in-C who had made himself an expert on railways. The proportion of deserters on mobilisation, predicted at 13 per cent, in fact reached less than 1.5 per cent. Morale, both in the Army and the Nation, had never been higher.[17]

For all the success of France's mobilisation in 1914, the military reforms of the *Réveil National* had come very late in the day, and in some respects the rot of the preceding two decades had penetrated too deeply. Particularly was this so as regards the quality of the High Command, and its doctrine of warfare – or, rather, its lack of a doctrine. During the critical years before 1914, the gospel of the offensive – *L'attaque à outrance* – had impregnated the French Army from top to bottom. It found its ultimate prophet in Colonel de Grandmaison, Chief of the *Troisième Bureau* (Operations) of the General Staff, who expounded such extravagant, semi-mystical rubbish as:

> In the offensive, imprudence is the best of assurances ... Let us go even to excess, and that will perhaps not be far enough ... For the attack only two things are necessary: to know where the enemy is and to decide what to do. What the enemy intends to do is of no consequence.[18]

Little study was make of the success of defence in such campaigns as the American Civil War, or the Boer War; while it was symptomatic that in 1913 some 300 books on war were published in Germany, to only fifty in France. In 1909 a senior representative of the General Staff had thanked God that the Army had no heavy artillery: 'The strength of the French Army is in the lightness of its guns.' So it went to war with few cannon heavier than the famous '75; brilliant on the *attaque à outrance* across open country, but hopeless for the trench-warfare that was to dominate the Western Front from the winter of 1914 onwards.

Of course, the *attaque à outrance* principle stemmed to some extent from the lessons derived from 1870, where the French Army was deemed to have failed through being too defensive-minded; at the same time, it also harked back to those respectably Republican precepts of 1792, of Danton's '*encore de l'audace, toujours de l'audace*'. Either way this was a reactive, or emotional, rather than a rational interpretation of history. Douglas Porch,[19] however, argues – and I think rather convincingly – that, for the origins of the lethal de Grandmaison school, one should scrutinise most carefully the damage done to the French Army's promotional system by General André's interference in the early 1900s. The fault was that the French Army had no consistent doctrine in 1914 and the *attaque à outrance* was only filling a vacuum: 'any army [says Porch] as riven by political and social strife and internal doubt as the post-1900 French army was simply not capable of formulating or applying a tactical doctrine'.[20] It had, furthermore, been André's fixed belief in the absence of a doctrine that permitted everyone to 'select a system in harmony with his own character, energy, temperament, aptitudes'.[21] Clearly an absurd notion, this took root when – in 1901 – André had abolished general inspections, thereby eliminating an important element of central control and standardisation. When Joffre was chosen as Chief-of-Staff in 1911 (in part because, as a sapper who had served most of his career in the colonies, he could safely be assumed to know nothing of military theory and would make an excellent figurehead), he tried hard to create a coherent war doctrine. But the system had defeated him, and the Joffre reforms foundered on the rocks of impoverished army leadership that came as the ineluctable consequence of André and the politicians tampering with army promotion. Thus, in 1914, concludes Porch:

> The Radical Republic got the army it deserved – a characterless leadership bolstered by a bureaucratic general staff, largely out of touch with the men it controlled.[22]

We all know what happened that terrible August of 1914. Under the French General Staff's disastrous Plan XVII, four out of five French armies, totalling 800 000 men, charged straight forward, with the main impetus directed towards the lost territories; objective, the Rhine.

True to de Grandmaison, the *deuxième bureau* had not troubled itself unduly to find out what the enemy's intentions might be. Marching to the Schlieffen Plan, these intentions in fact were to sweep through Belgium, around the left flank of the advancing French Army, wheel eastwards to the west of Paris, and then roll the French up from the rear. Attacking with extraordinary heroism into the German machine-guns, the French turned the stubble-fields of eastern France to bright carpets of red and blue – the red trousers selected, in preference to less conspicuous colours, by nationalists who thought red more helpful to morale in *l'attaque*. In the two weeks that the 'Battle of the Frontiers' lasted, Joffre lost 300 000 men and 4778 officers – one-tenth of France's total officer strength. Then the German steam-roller ran out of steam, and was brought to a halt within sight of the Eiffel Tower by the 'Miracle of the Marne'. By the autumn of 1914, a continuous static front had been established from Switzerland to the Belgian coast, which was to remain barely dented by either side, despite an appalling expenditure in lives, until the Ludendorff 'last-gasp' offensive of 1918. The horrors of trench warfare now began.[23]

During these grim days, two factors notably saved France; one was the remarkable patriotic compact, formed between all political parties on the eve of war, and called the *Union Sacrée*; the other was the portly and imperturbable figure of Joseph Césaire Joffre, of whom I remarked, not altogether inaccurately, in *The Price of Glory* that, 'the war was very nearly lost with him, but . . . would almost certainly have been lost without him'. As already noted, Joffre was a sapper who had spent his career in the colonies and was therefore a talented organiser rather than a strategist, or tactician. Which indeed he was not. It is also of relevance to our story that his appointment (in 1911) came more for his qualities as a 'good Republican' (and poor church-goer!) than for any military brilliance. At the same time, making Joffre Chief-of-the-General-Staff, the War Minister, Messimy – in an attempt to reverse the debasement of the High Command he inherited from André – had created a new post in the military hierarchy, and which carried immense prerogatives in time of war. Possibly Joffre's greatest attributes were his utterly unshakeable nerves and almost inhuman calm – something which a shaken France badly needed, and which he displayed equally when assaulted by the enemy, or by critical politicians. Standing orders were that (not unlike Monty) he should never, repeat never, be woken whatever military disaster might have transpired; he loathed the telephone, and at the height of the crisis of the Marne he refused to have even President Poincaré put through to him.

Apart from his doctrinal shortcomings, Joffre's chief defect was his apparent powerlessness to weed out the de Grandmaison satraps, and the mediocre, from the *Grand Quartier Général* (GQG). Well isolated in its palace at Chantilly, GQG lived amid an atmosphere of back-stabbing intrigue and jockeying for position that was reminiscent of the Court of Louis XV at Versailles. It also maintained its own vast propaganda system, designed to deceive the outside world, and thus perpetuate its own existence; but this often resulted in its deceiving itself, too. The Government, partially discredited and its power considerably trimmed after the first disasters of 1914, found it increasingly difficult to intervene in this mighty, sealed brotherhood that was the GQG. One sees here the beginning of one of those remarkable swings and reversals in French history; from being unpopular, under-privileged and at the total whim of government, as it had been from 1900 onwards, with war the Army became all-popular and all-powerful. The roles were completely reversed.[24]

I mentioned the political *Union Sacrée* coalition, formed to prosecute the war. At its head, symbol of reawakened patriotism, was a staunch *revanchist* from Lorraine,

Raymond Poincaré, elected President in 1914, and with the country whole-heartedly behind him. The *Union Sacrée* was backed by politicians of all hues – even the left-wing pacifists, despite the tragic assassination of the great Socialist leader, Jaurès, on the eve of war – showing a degree of unity not seen in France since Napoleon I (and nor was it to be seen again in the Third, Fourth or even Republics). The unique mood of the *Union Sacrée* had been set in 1911, with a declaration by a Radical Deputy, André Hesse: 'When the guns begin to speak, it is best that the politicians keep quiet.'[25]

All this meant that, like Britain in 1940, France now had a war body that could prosecute the war, and accept appalling losses without being turned out, and this would continue for over two years. But it also meant that the political had abdicated power to the military. As the Germans approached Paris, the Government left hastily for Bordeaux. Exaggerated rumours of the deputies' Capuan luxuries there soon reached the front, and the repute of the politicians collapsed.

Meanwhile, never since Bonaparte had one Frenchman been so popular (or so all-powerful) as Joffre. Carloads of gifts, boxes of chocolates, cigars and fan mail rolled in daily. Joffre himself had encouraged the Government's departure, seeing clearly that it would 'favour and develop the omnipotence of the GQG'.[26] At the very beginning Joffre had got his superior, War Minister Messimy, to agree docilely to leaving all operations 'to the military technicians'.[27] He noted, 'I may say that from this moment, the minister did nothing without consulting me.' Although Joffre came under some sharp parliamentary attacks for the first reverses, with Clemenceau – in the old vein – attributing these to Joffre's appointment of generals 'from the Jesuit warrens'[28] (meaning notably de Castelnau), Messimy's successor, Millerand, proved even more dedicated in defending the authority of the High Command.

In 1915, there was a struggle – won by Joffre, aided by Millerand – to deny access to the front to inspection teams, sent by a parliament increasingly apprehensive at the continued futile blood-letting. When, in May 1915, General Pédoya, head of the Army Commission, refused to give an explanation of why he wished to visit the lines, he was threatened with arrest if he proceeded. Via a liaison officer, Joffre told his Minister,

> He may come and see me, if that pleases him, but I request him not to go where there is fighting. That would trouble people.[29]

Even the arch-patriot President, Poincaré, complained sadly that Millerand, 'one of my oldest friends, aspires to leave me less power than a senator or a deputy; I must not confer with a chief of a service without his previous consent'.[30] Which, in effect, meant Joffre's consent.

Now all this took place in 1915, a year of blundering and murderously wasteful attacks on the German lines in what Joffre called his strategy of *grignotage*, or 'nibbling-away' at the enemy. It has also been described as 'trying to bite through a steel door with badly fitting false teeth'.[31] In Artois, in May, the French lost 102000 men, more than twice as many as the defenders, for an advance of two miles. In September, they lost 242000. Each battle had failed largely due to the lack of the heavy guns so despised by de Grandmaison and his disciples. By the end of 1915, France had now lost 50 per cent of her regular officers while her dead already approached the total Britain was to lose in the whole war. There were conspiracies to replace Joffre with Sarrail, known as the 'red Republican general', apparently with political connivance by Sarrail himself. But Joffre caught word of the plot; Sarrail was shipped off to Macedonia. Premier Briand was replaced by Viviani, Millerand by General Galliéni. But Joffre seemed unsackable. In fact, on 2 December, in addition to his directly controlling the whole Western Front, the Near

East was also put under his control. Despite everything, Joffre had reached the peak of his power; become a virtual dictator, he had greater authority over the French Army than any general since Bonaparte, and – by the beginning of the 1916 campaign – he was brought close to being a supra-national generalissimo, co-ordinating Allied operations, like Eisenhower in World War II. Meanwhile, the Government, having abdicated its authority, had no means of intervening to stop the carnage on the Western Front – even if it had an alternative strategy to Joffre; which it had not.[32]

1916 was the year of Verdun and the Somme, the bloodiest of the war. Joffre had planned an Anglo-French 'Big Push' astraddle the River Somme for the summer; but the German leader, Erich von Falkenhayn, beat him to the draw by launching a surprise attack in February on France's most famous fortress. The tragic story of Verdun, history's longest and most costly battle, has been told elsewhere; all that needs to be said here is that the High Command was caught napping, and then committed France to a heroic, but Pyrrhic defence of a place that was full of moral, but doubtful strategic import. Psychological and political considerations were allowed to take precedence over good military sense; although the Government was barely consulted over the higher issues involved. This was, in itself, fresh indication of just how far political influence over the military had slipped since 1914. In March the War Minister, now General Galliéni, totally disenchanted with Joffre, recommended to the Government:

1. Put the High Command back in the place where it belongs and withdraw from it all of its conerns except the direction of military operations;
2. Restore to the minister his administrative control.[33]

But Galliéni died before any reforms could be introduced.
Then, in June, during the worst week of the battle, the

Union Sacrée nearly broke down when the Government held its first Secret Session of the war. The first speaker was one ex-sergeant André Maginot, who had lost a leg at Verdun, and would give his name to a large piece of real estate in the inter-war era. He fiercely attacked GQG for its 'unpreparedness and inertia'. Maginot was followed by Abel Ferry, the youngest and most critical member of the Parliamentary Army Commission, who noted pungently: 'There are two Frances, two Frances who struggle separately, each in its own zone. There are two ministries: a Ministry of War in Paris and another ministry in the zone of the armies at Chantilly.[34]

Falkenhayn's aim to 'bleed the French Army white' at Verdun came within an inch of success; but it also bled the German Army disastrously. Lasting ten months, the casualties totalled over 700 000 for both sides, of which substantially more than half were French. Joffre's days were numbered. In December 1916, he was kicked upstairs and then quietly shuffled out of the corridors of power.

Out of the hell of Verdun emerged two contenders for the succession. One was Pétain, the defensive general *par excellence*, who – with his maxim 'firepower kills' – was one of the few genuinely to practise parsimony with his men's lives. As much as he was beloved by the soldiers, he was distrusted by the politicians because of his virulent, and poorly concealed contempt for them. Pétain had once mortally offended even Poincaré by the acid remark that 'nobody was better placed than the President himself to be aware that France was neither led nor governed'. Pétain's view of politicians was, again, partly a legacy of the Combes-André era, and it would also exert an important influence a generation later. Thus, in 1917, Pétain was by-passed for Nivelle, the attacking general who had coined the immortal phrase at Verdun, '*Ils ne passeront pas!*' Apart from his success in the relief of Verdun, Nivelle had two points in his favour: he was a Protestant, and he could get on with politicians – in contrast with Pétain and the other possible contenders, the reactionary Catholics, Foch and Castelnau.[35]

If the replacement of Joffre by Nivelle suggests that the spirit of General André still hovered unexorcised among French politicians, it also heralded the beginnings of a reassertion of governmental authority over the military for the first time since 1914. In the spring of 1917, Nivelle led the French Army to disaster and mutiny on the Chemin des Dames. Nivelle refused at first to resign – an unthinkable situation, suggestive of Government debility. After some humiliation, it was forced to swallow its pride and call in Pétain. Broken by the losses at Verdun, followed by the Chemin des Dames, and deeply influenced by revolution in Russia, a major part of the French Army was in open mutiny, with divisions actually threatening to march on Paris. Never before had the French *poilu* come to feel so isolated from the rest of the nation. As one of the characters in Henri Barbusse's great anti-war novel, *Le Feu*, comments bitterly while on leave, 'We are divided into two foreign countries. The front, over there, where there is too much misery, and the rear, here, where there is too much contentment.'

In quelling the mutinies, improving conditions at the front and restoring morale, Pétain – as *le Médécin de l'Armée* – made perhaps his greatest contribution to France. He was ably aided by Painlevé, first War Minister and later Premier, who pressed the purge of civilian defeatists and 'Fifth Columnists', while working with Lloyd-George to set up the long-needed Supreme War Council. One of the few, but fundamental disagreements between the two concerned their analysis of the causes behind the mutinies; characteristically the soldier blamed political shortcomings, while Painlevé, the Socialist politician, placed the responsibility on the military. Otherwise, however, this relationship represented a unique honeymoon period, with the political and military working in harmony together for the first, and last, time in the war.

Finally, and very much at the eleventh hour, France produced her winning combination. US entry into the war in April 1917 had strengthened the tottering *Union Sacrée*, but – with Russia out of it and Ludendorff able to concentrate all on the west – the situation was still desperate. Parliamentarians had long feared that if Clemenceau, the ferocious Jacobin Radical, were allowed to get his hands on the power he had so long been denied, that would be tantamount to creating a dictatorship. But now circumstances brooked no alternative. In November 1917, the 76-year-old 'Tiger' became Premier, with a simple programme:

'Home policy? I wage war! Foreign Policy? I wage war! All the time I wage war.'[36]

This even took priority over his lifelong distrust of the Army's conservative and clerical establishment, and he now lent his considerable force to crushing the wobbly Left, his own former allies. But it was also Clemenceau who coined anew Talleyrand's maxim: 'War is much too serious a thing to be left to the military.'[37] At a meeting of the Supreme War Council on 14 March 1918 there was a fiery exchange between Foch and Clemenceau over the use of the new General Reserve, with Clemenceau eventually shouting down Foch: 'Be quiet: I am the representative of France here!'[38]

On 21 March, Ludendorff launched his devastating all-out attempt to break the Allied front – and very nearly succeeded. Foch was now, at last, brought in as Allied Supreme Commander. Clemenceau managed to enrage him with his acid remark: '*Eh bien,* now you have got the position you wanted so much!' to which Foch retorted, 'You give me a lost battle and you ask me to win it. I consent, and you think you are making me a present.'[39] Nevertheless, despite his personal antipathy and his conviction that Catholicism was to Foch what whiskey had been to Ulysses S. Grant,[40] Clemenceau's respect for his indomitable fighting spirit took precedence over all else. '*C'est un bougre*', he declared with grudging admiration after Foch's famous fighting rejoinder to Pétain at Doullens during the darkest days of March 1918.

> You aren't fighting? I would fight without a break. I would fight in front of Amiens. I would fight in Amiens. I would fight behind Amiens, I would fight all the time.[41]

Thereafter Clemenceau contrived to gear policy so as to be at one with the strategy of victory. He backed Foch staunchly through that terrible spring of 1918, and through the summer when the tide at last turned: 'We must have confidence in Foch and Pétain, those two great chiefs who are so complementary to each other,'[42] he declared on 5 June. That summer Foch justified the politician's confidence, showing himself to be master of the integrated offensive, switching fronts rapidly as the great German horde began to reach the end of its tether, then moving into his massive across-the-board attack:

> *Tout le monde à la bataille!*

Thus had the wheel turned. France began the war with the politicians of the *Union Sacrée* coalition, in their weakness, granting Joffre *carte blanche* to run what amounted to almost a military dictatorship; it ended with a powerful Jacobin Republican premier, with all but total powers, fully in control of both parliament and the military. Despite the enormous popularity of Foch – and Pétain – when armistice came in November 1918, France had probably never been in less of a mood to follow 'the man on horseback'.[43]

III

Collapse 1940, 1919–40

A generation that has taken a thrashing is always followed
by one that deals out the thrashing.

Bismarck[1]

As peace came in November 1918, Foch declared to
Clemenceau: 'My task is over, yours is beginning'.[2] The
truth was not quite so simple as all that; for Foch would go
on fighting fiercely for a tough peace treaty, which would
often bring him to trespass upon the political prerogatives
of Clemenceau.

Between the years 1919 and 1940, the military scene
is dominated by four main figures: apart from Foch and
Pétain, they were Weygand (Foch's wartime Chief-of-
Staff) and Gamelin (who, in 1914, had been a staff officer
at Joffre's GQG). Thus this interwar period came to be
heavily overshadowed by the experience of the First
World War; from which, as everyone knows, the wrong
lessons were drawn, with calamitous results. The defen-
sive-mindedness of French doctrine, a pendulum swing
from the *attaque à outrance* of 1914, would lead to the
building of the Maginot line and a doctrine of static
defence, at a time when Hitler's generals across the Rhine

would be concentrating on tanks and aircraft for the *Blitzkrieg* lightning war.

But what concerns us here has to be the interplay of these military leaders – and their plans – with the politicians of the Third Republic.

One may start with Foch and his struggle against Clemenceau for a Peace Treaty that would give France a strong foothold on the Rhine. Already in the days before victory, in September 1918, the Foch/Clemenceau entente had taken an acrid turn that boded ill for the future. Critical of Foch's deployment of the American Army, Clemenceau had complained that the generalissimo did not 'know how to enforce his will', and added menacingly, 'You will have to answer to France for it.' Foch, piqued, and his head having been perhaps somewhat swollen by receipt of his Marshal's baton the previous month, counter-attacked with the reminder that, as Allied Generalissimo, 'Constitutionally, I am not under your orders.' This provoked an acid retort from The Tiger 'not to try that game'.[3] The next row came in October over armistice terms; Haig wanted to moderate these, so as to speed an end to the fighting. Foch was bitterly opposed; the British and Americans were upset, both by Foch's hard line and his intervention in policy. Clemenceau came down on their side. On 16 October, Foch wrote to Clemenceau already calling for a permanent French occupation of the left bank of the Rhine, which was a German-speaking area hitherto an integral part of the German Reich. A snubbing reply came back from Clemenceau: 'Your business is war; but everything pertaining to peace, our Rhineland policy ... concerns ourselves exclusively. We will not suffer you to interfere in these matters.'[4] Foch's view, one which would not commend itself to the Anglo-Saxon way of thinking,[5] was that, 'War, like peace, is not a duality but an integer. It does not call for a military compartment here and a civilian compartment there. The two are closely combined.'

Thus, as the Great War ended, a new war opened between the world's most powerful – and popular – soldier and the Premier of France. Foch returned to the attack in February 1919 with a memorandum expounding the dangers of not occupying the Rhineland.

> Germany, he declared, could by-pass France's natural defences in a few days by invading Belgium and Luxembourg; if the first battle was lost by the French Army, continental Europe would fall into the hands of the German Army, and it would then be difficult for the American and British forces to establish bridgeheads in Europe. Consequently the Rhine was the only possible frontier, not only for France, but for the whole group of western countries.[6]

There are obvious similarities here in recent times with the Israeli Army's case for hanging on to the West Bank, while 1940 could be seen as entirely vindicating Foch's line – at least in purely military terms. But, at the same time, one might also find an instance of the soldier seeing only the military implications, while being blinkered to the wider political scene. Clemenceau saw these wider implications and placed all his money on an 'automatic and immediate alliance' with the United States and Great Britain, as a better bet than a permanent occupation of the Rhineland guaranteed only by an isolated French Army. Despite the stern *revanchist* views he had held ever since 1871, Clemenceau now spoke of Germany as 'a country of sixty million inhabitants ... We have to live with them.'[7]

After the appalling losses suffered by France, 1.3 million dead, or 27 per cent of all men between the ages of eighteen and twenty-seven, the highest mortality rate of all the combatant nations, Clemenceau like all his countrymen was, nevertheless, determined there should be no 'soft' peace for the defeated nation. Initially he was prepared to back Foch's case; but *not* if it were to lead to a breach with Woodrow Wilson and Lloyd George. After a month of hard talking, Clemenceau was forced to abandon the principle of Rhineland occupation, accepting instead its permanent demilitarisation.

Foch was appalled, predicting (accurately as it turned out) that ratification of any Franco-American military alliance by the US Senate would be 'a very uncertain contingency', and he now sought to contest his Government's policy by every means. He threatened to walk out of the Peace Conference; he refused to transmit orders for conveyance of the German delegation; he refused to leave a session of the Supreme War Council, after Clemenceau had called on the military advisers to retire. (An *opéra bouffe* scene ensued, with Clemenceau wailing to Wilson, 'I don't know what to do, he won't leave!', and the day saved by a typical British compromise when Foreign Secretary Balfour proposed, 'I suggest we have tea!')[8] Then Foch, quite improperly, gave an explosive – but prophetic – interview with the London *Daily Mail*,[9] vigorously attacking the Peace Treaty in preparation:

> What was it that saved the Allies at the beginning of the war? asked Foch. Russia. Well, on whose side will Russia be in the future? With us or with the Germans? . . . The Allied armies? Where will the Allied armies be? The British army will be in Canada, in Australia, in New Zealand. The American armies will be in the United States ... And next time, remember, the Germans will make no mistake. They will break through Northern France and will seize the Channel ports as a base of operations against England.

Amen!

Like Truman versus Macarthur during the Korean War, Clemenceau contemplated sacking his insubordinate general. But, unlike Truman, his political base was not firm enough; Foch and his supporting generals were too popular. Instead, Clemenceau took the course of keeping Foch uninformed to the point of disingenuousness. His motives for this, for not discussing compromises with a man he knew would only try to sabotage them, were not unreasonable, but unwise in that they only exacerbated the grave split between these two ardent patriots of France, with unhappy results for her future. Foch's disaffection alienated both Lloyd George and Wilson. On receiving Foch's second memorandum on annexation of the Rhineland, in January 1919, Lloyd George had commented with the warning: 'On my last trip to Paris my strongest impression was the statue of Strasbourg in its veil of mourning. Do not allow Germany to erect such a statue.[10]

At one of the ensuing Peace Treaty sessions he propounded a clear-cut Anglo-Saxon attitude; although the concurrence of the military was essential in time of war, said Lloyd George:

> In the domain of the statesman, they are the very last ones I would consult. I admire and love Marshal Foch very much, but on political questions he is an infant. I would not take his advice as to the means of assuring nations the most effective security.[11]

When Foch, in April, refused to transmit Clemenceau's order for the conveyance of the German delegations, it was an outraged Woodrow Wilson who declared: 'I will not entrust the American Army to a general who does not obey his government.'[12] Back in Washington, the episode did certainly not go unmarked by the increasingly hostile US Senate. At the 6 May Plenary Session of the peace conference, Bonar Law, one of the British delegates, echoed Wilson: 'If an English general took such an attitude *vis-à-vis* his government, he would be dismissed within fifteen minutes,'[13] to which Clemenceau gave this revealing answer: 'However much I regret the Marshal's attitude, we must not forget that he led our soldiers to victory.'[14] The fundamental difference between French and British views on the military in politics could not have been stated more positively.

Thwarted at the conference table, Foch – never one to say die – switched fronts more directly but also more deviously, to the Rhineland itself. There Foch had a doughty lieutenant in the shape of General Charles Mangin, nicknamed 'the butcher of Verdun' and hero of the summer of 1918, and now commanding the army of occupation at Mainz. True to his background as an officer of the colonial army, Mangin ran the zone like a feudal fiefdom, permitting the minimum interference from Paris. ('Obedience was not made for him' was Clemenceau's view of Mangin.)[15] Needing little encouragement, but with Foch's full support, Mangin became deeply involved in the Rhineland separatist movement – granting it all possible aid, moral and material, without informing the Government or obtaining its sanction.

French interest in Rhenish separatism had a lengthy history, going back to Napoleon, Louis XIV and well beyond. One of several inflammatory books published in 1915[16] claimed that the Rhenish states 'belonged to us in the Celtic, Gallo-Roman, Merovingian and Carolingian epochs. German on the surface, their population, especially in the countryside, is deeply Gallic in soul and blood.' It might also have added, Catholic. Springing up in the last days of the war, the Rhineland separatist movement wanted to establish a Catholic state, free of Protestant Prussian control, and closely associated with France. One of its leaders was a Dr Hans Adam Dorten, a Düsseldorf lawyer who had also fought through the hell of Verdun (on the German side), and another Catholic Rhinelander who toyed with it – though he was assiduous in denying this when he came to power and fame three decades later – was Dr Konrad Adenauer, first Chancellor of the German Federal Republic. In May 1919 Dorten launched an ill-conceived putsch, backed by Mangin with Foch behind him. The British (haunted by Napoleonic memories) promptly repudiated the new 'state', but it was Clemenceau who administered the *coup de grâce*, censuring the maladroit Mangin, in whose face the abortive putsch had blown up: no French commander, he declared, had the authority 'to pronounce . . . in advance on the merit of a new political constitution for a country which he controls'.[17] Shortly after the Peace Treaty was safely signed on 28 June 1919 Clemenceau had Mangin quietly shuffled out of his command.

To Clemenceau, Foch's involvement in the Catholic Rhineland conspiracy naturally re-aroused – and, to a large extent, confirmed – his worst suspicions about the consequences of clerical influences within the Army. Conspicuously Foch absented himself from the Hall of Mirrors on the day the Treaty was signed, and, when visiting the USA two years later, aged 70 and feeling his age, he remarked bitterly, 'Clemenceau has lost the peace.' In fact, it might have been truer to say that, through the uncompromising discord between the great soldier and the great politician, France had lost the peace. One must be careful not to overstate the influence that Foch's 'disobedience', and his machinations in the Rhineland had upon US refusal to ratify Versailles – but certainly they cannot have been negligible. Perhaps I have devoted too much time to this issue, but it seems both to have much relevance to our theme, as well as to the essential tragedy of the interwar era that led to France's desperate position of 1940. One last point; though the warnings of Foch prophesied with much deadly accuracy what was to come, in strategic terms his urging the importance of a static defence line along the Rhine showed a fundamental misappreciation of the new nature of mechanised warfare. This was particularly ironic, considering that Foch – the supreme exponent of the successful offensive – had been, in 1918, the first warlord to launch attacks of massed tanks, and aircraft.[18]

In domestic politics, that miraculous wartime truce between all parties and classes, the *Union Sacrée*, barely survived the Armistice. 'The War is dead. Long live the War,' declared the trades unions of Bourges.[19] The great victory celebrations of July 1919 were boycotted by a new constellation of the far Left, of Communists and extreme Socialists; it was symbolic of the vast chasm suddenly appearing between Right and Left, the deepest since 1871, which was to bedevil the nation right through to the catastrophe of 1940. The causes are not difficult to itemise: on the Left, apart from the reaction that inevitably follows the social and economic deprivations of war, and the fact that there was no titanic figure like Jaurès to provide a note of moderation, above all Russia's October Revolution of 1917 had struck more powerful chords among the workers of France than of any other of the victorious nations. Among the interventionist forces in Russia, it was the French sailors at Odessa who first raised the flag of mutiny. Taken out of moth-balls, the colours of the Communards were unfurled and waved again. During Poincaré's occupation of the Ruhr in 1923 (carried out after Germany had defaulted on reparations), the *Jeunes Communistes* deluged army conscripts with manifestos.[20] 'In no circumstances,' they proclaimed, 'will your bayonets pierce the breasts of the rebelling German workers ... Set out for the Army in order to be soldiers of Communism.' The Party line of the 1920s specified, 'It is better to shoot a French general than a foreign soldier,'[21] so it was hardly surprising that fear, and reaction, was provoked among army officers. Politically, on the Right, the bourgeois, property-owning classes closed their ranks against this new threat; in the first post-war elections of November 1919 a newly created right-of-centre *Bloc National Républicain* swept up nearly three-quarters of the seats in the Assembly – the first time since 1871 that it had turned so decisively to the Right.[22]

Soon we find another of those violent swings that characterise the relationship between the French Army and *la Nation*. With Alsace-Lorraine safely returned to the fold, the spiritual goad of *la Revanche* evaporated, and, as revulsion against the horrors of such battlefields as Verdun replaced adulation of its legends of heroism, so there

emerged a new mood of anti-militarism even more reson-
ant than that of the Dreyfus era. In the late 1920s and
1930s anti-war writings by such giants of the intellectual
Left as Gide, Eluard, Aragon and Romain Rolland – and,
even more, Henri Barbussé's *Le Feu* – dominated France's
literary scene, while films like Renoir's immortal master-
piece *La Grande Illusion* made an immeasurable impact.
With an extraordinary speed that was disheartening for
the Army, it suddenly became unfashionable again. At St
Cyr, the first advice given young cadets was to wear
civilian clothes whenever they went into certain districts
of Paris: 'Among the masses, we were considered the
enemy ... In bourgeois circles, we were considered
imbeciles.'[23] Throughout the twenties there were massive
resignations from the Army among the moneyed
bourgeoisie and aristocracy; thus its outlook became
progressively that of what, in the 1950s, might have been
identified as the Poujadist middle classes. As financial
crises, followed by the world depression, bit deeper and
deeper, so the social standing of officers sank. Already by
1925, the saver of 1918 would have lost 60 per cent of his
capital. By 1935, a major commanding a battalion received only £16 a month (even in the underpaid British
Army of that date, a major's basic pay was £53). Grim
stories appeared regularly in the press about officers
driving taxis by night, or wrapping up parcels in a department store. Where, then, lay the glory of an Army career?

For their plight, army officers instantly blamed the
politicians for letting the currency be wrecked – as well as
letting the Allies wreck the peace – and out of this grew
increasingly strong anti-parliamentary sentiments. Hand
in hand went a feeling that, now the German threat had
been (at least temporarily) removed, Bolshevism was
Enemy No. 1. In the military mind Bolshevism abroad
and defeatism at home were closely linked; result, a
constant surveillance of all suspected of allegiance to the
French Communist Party (PCF). From the early twenties

a kind of folk hero of the military archetype emerged in the shape of Maxime Weygand, sent to Warsaw to help the Pilsudski Poles (successfully) against the assault of the wicked Soviets.[24]

Always controversial, Weygand even entered the world enveloped in mystery; was he the bastard of Belgian King Leopold II, or of ill-fated Emperor Maximilian, or his wife, the crazed Carlotta? Whichever, he instinctively donned the attributes of the aristocrat; was ultra-conservative, and Catholic ('Up to his neck in priests, naturally,' was Clemenceau's damning comment).[25] Deeply affected by *The Affair* as a young captain, Weygand remained unconvinced of Dreyfus's innocence. Throughout 1914–18 he held no active command (a factor of note when the top post came to him in the crisis of 1940), but was the brilliant Chief-of-Staff to Foch, with a reputedly almost intuitive understanding of the thought processes of his chief. Clemenceau regarded Weygand as the 'better intellectual part of Foch' and (together with Lloyd George) suspected him of being the political *eminence grise* during the intrigues over the Rhineland. (This was a view shared by Lloyd George, who remarked after a particularly sulphurous session on 16 June 1919, 'I see him constantly whispering into the ear of the Marshal and telling him what to say.' Woodrow Wilson had added: 'The danger is to leave the fate of Europe in the hands of General Weygand ... I cannot consent to that.')[26] Meanwhile, the Left fearful then of an Army coup centred round Foch, instinctively saw Weygand at its political hub.

Such fears may have been grossly unfounded; nevertheless, they had a serious influence on relations between the military and political when Weygand was appointed Chief-of-the-General Staff on 3 January 1930[27] in succession to the retiring Marshal Pétain, and – one year later – Vice President of the CSG, Inspector-General, and thus Generalissimo designate in the event of war. The Socialist coerced the Minister of War, ex-Sergeant Maginot, into imposing as assistant – and political counterweight – to Weygand General Maurice Gamelin, who, as a protégé of such good Republican generals as Joffre and 'Red' Sarrail, was considered 'sound'. For the next five years, until his retirement, Weygand was in constant conflict with his civil superiors. First, he did his best to sabotage the Disarmament Conference of 1934, on the ground that disarmament jeopardised France's whole defence posture. Weygand may well have been dead right; nevertheless this surely constituted an interference in the policy of Government. Secondly, he fought a bitter struggle – reminiscent of those of the pre-1914 years – to have conscription raised from one to two years. It was not won until after Weygand's departure the two-year term was restored by War Minister Maurin in 1935, but here he was on sounder ground. The *années creuses* – years when the birthrate tumbled because of the First War – resulted in a grave loss of military manpower, and the one-year service was deemed insufficient to train NCOs. (Notable was the fact that, at Sedan in 1940, the reservist divisions that collapsed did so not least because of a dearth of good NCOs.) Another quarrel broke out over War Minister Daladier's elimination in 1933 of 5000 officers, or one-sixth of the establishment, over which neither Weygand nor Gamelin was properly consulted. In both cases, the Socialist Herriot Government had acted primarily out of economic, but also *political* considerations, to reach decisions of top military concern.[28] For instance, Daladier, when War Minister, spotted a possible electoral benefit from fixed defences on the frontier, in that they might reduce the need for unpopular military service.

One needs to mention here the famous, ill-starred Maginot Line. France's post-war army had been virtually created under three major laws of 1927 and 1928, and in 1930 Weygand had inherited from Pétain what was to be essentially its shape and doctrine until the Second World War. It is hard for us, blinded by the tragedy – and disgrace – which subsequently overtook him, to recall the immense reverence with which France regarded Pétain in the post-1918 era, exceeding even that accorded Foch. (For example, in a 1935 newspaper referendum enquiring whom the French would most like as a dictator, Pétain came top.) From 1920 through to 1936 it was thus Pétain, with his old ideas of defensive doctrine that had served so well in 1914–18, who continued to dominate France's military thought. The day after Weygand's accession – but obviously still under the aegis of Pétain – the French Assembly, denied the protective glacis of the Rhineland sought by Foch, voted to construct a Great Wall along the eastern frontier.

The Maginot Line was motivated by expediency; France knew she simply could not defend herself again at the cost in human lives of 1914–18. As a young lieutenant had scrawled in his journal shortly before he was killed at Verdun: 'They will not be able to make us do it again another day; that would be to misconstrue the price of our effort,'[29] and few Frenchmen of the post-war generation felt they could 'do' Verdun again. But putting the expedient, that which is *acceptable*, first, is not always the best way of ensuring the defence a country needs. Nevertheless, poor Sergeant Maginot's much-maligned Line might well have been all right on the day; if only it had been extended to the Channel coast, and if it had been backed up by adequate mobile troops. *If only*. By 1935, however, the eighty-seven miles already completed had far exceeded parliamentary estimates; which, in political terms, meant that drastic economies had to be imposed on the Army elsewhere. So something like the Nott defence cuts of 1982 hit the *couverture* force, for which Weygand considered two-year conscription essential. (1935 also happened to be the year that Hitler began rearming the *Wehrmacht* with *Panzer* units specially designed to penetrate fixed defences.)

There was, additionally, behind the 'Maginot Line

Mentality', another purely political consideration that echoes all the way back through the epochs we have covered so far in these lectures – and will again onwards to 1970. The Line accorded well with the long-held Republican principles of the Socialist/Radical élite currently in power, of the citizen-army defensively deployed. What did not appeal to them were notions of a small, professional corps of mechanised, offensive units. This was what, between 1933 and 1935, a young major called Charles de Gaulle had been advocating as the best means of deterring German aggression – backed by a political maverick of diminutive stature, but great courage, Paul Reynaud. To the doctrinaire Left, de Gaulle's hundred-thousand sounded just like the sort of force that might be used for strike-breaking and helping the Right oppress the workers, as in the bad old days of Louis Napoleon and 1906, rather than for dealing with any external enemy. An *armée de coup d'état*, was the immediate reaction of Léon Blum and the *Front Populaire* – backed by Daladier the Radical, who declared: 'We do not want any professional shock Army, more dangerous than any one could believe for the security of the country.'[30] For his audacity in publishing *Vers l'Armée de Métier* de Gaulle was struck from the 1936 promotion list. It was more reassuring for deputies to hear War Minister Maurin tell them[31] that, having built the Maginot Line, 'Who could believe us foolish enough to sally out in front of this barrier, in search of heaven knows what adventure?'[32]

At the other end of the political spectrum, Weygand also condemned the de Gaulle/Reynaud thesis: 'What a hotbed of Communism, this troop of mechanics,[33] was his scathing comment. But his opposition was also not entirely divorced from a somewhat out-dated view of modern war; while he misled the French public into deeper complacency by declarations like the following: 'As for the mechanised reserve ... Nothing needs to be created, as all of it exists.'[34] This was a palpable untruth; only the 1st

DLM, Light Mechanised Division, no match for Hitler's heavy *Panzers*, had actually been formed.[35] The Germans, although they derived greater benefits from the more original and profounder writings of Britain's prophet-without-honour, Basil Liddell Hart, also took the right course in opting for a small *armée de métier* in the early days of the 'Black *Reichswehr*'; albeit that this was imposed on them by Versailles. As Rommel's former staff chief, General Speidel remarked after 1945, 'This gave us an army of cadres ... if we had had an army of conscripts, we would have been drowned.'[36]

There was one other direction of great moment where Weygand's powerful political tenets may have influenced, banefully, the course of French policy. As early as 1932–3, Weygand saw the urgent need to separate Russia from Germany, but his detestation of Bolshevism made him wary of forming any close, or permanent, military links with the USSR. From then on, increasingly, he viewed the Soviet Union and the French Communist Party as a graver threat than war with Nazi Germany; sentiments which the French Right came to echo in the late thirties with its slogan of *'plutôt Hitler que Blum'*.[37] Here Weygand in his hostility towards Russia typified the Army's attitude, in which he was extensively backed by his successor, Gamelin. Who knows, had Weygand applied his considerable political influence differently, could Franco–Soviet military co-operation have saved Poland in 1939, instead of the sullen Ribbentrop–Molotov Pact which doomed her, and made the Second World War inevitable? (In his writings Weygand indeed reveals a fairly constant respect for the Fascist states, Italy and Spain; Mussolini he praised as the regenerator of Italy's soul, Franco a 'chief animated by ardent patriotism'.)

At the end of 1933, Weygand had reached an open break with the Government over its conscription policy. Anti-parliamentary sentiment had never been stronger in the Army. Under a rousing caption of 'Military catastrophe or rearmament' the right-wing *Revue Hebdomadaire* published a series of apparently inspired articles, supporting all Weygand's theses and declaring that, because of the policies pursued by governments of the Left, 'France no longer enjoyed any protection on land.'[38] On 10 January 1934 *La Victoire* enquired challengingly: 'Who will be the chief to emerge in France as one has come forth in Italy and Germany,' to get rid of 'this impotent and corrupt regime?'[39] (The regime it referred to was the Chautemps Government, already tottering from the Stavisky scandal, and it fell two weeks later.) Rumours ran round Paris of a military coup, coupled with the name of Weygand. On the Right, even moderate conservatives talked fearfully of a left-wing plot to seize power. On 6 February 1934 passions overflowed in Paris. Some 40 000 demonstrators from such rightist and veterans' organisations as Colonel de la Rocque's *Croix de Feu*, the monarchist *Camelots du Roi* and the anti-Communist *Jennesses Patriotes*, marched on the Assembly. The police opened fire, twice; sixteen demonstrators were killed, and over a thousand policmen injured. The following day the new premier, Daladier, resigned rather than face further bloodshed. It was the first time since 1870 that a Government had been brought down by a Paris mob, and nothing like the bitterness between Right and Left had been seen since the Commune. Responding to 6 February, the Left closed ranks to form a 'common anti-Fascist' front. In May 1936, weeks after Hitler moved back into the demilitarised Rhineland, the *Front Populaire* swept into power under the leadership of Léon Blum. As the Second World War approached, France teetered on the brink of civil war.

that half the organisers were ex-officers, retired or still on the reserve – including one Marshal, Lyautey. They also disclosed an indirect link between the right-wing groups and Weygand. The general's contact-man was a Colonel Jean de Lattre de Tassigny, later to become France's great soldier-hero of the Second World War and a *Maréchal de France* himself – as well as, ironically, the man deputed by de Gaulle to arrest Weygand in Lindau in 1945. After 1934 a more disreputable body called the *Cagoule*, formed expressly to combat the Communists with underground violence, was proved to have a line even to Pétain, through a fanatical anti-Communist and anti-Parliamentarian on his staff called Commandant Loustaunau-Lacau. Though hitherto Pétain had kept glacially aloof from political intrigues, like Weygand he too had come to develop a contempt for the men of the Third Republic far exceeding his opinion that had so shocked President Poincaré in the First World War.[40]

In 1935, Weygand retired, angry and bitter, blaming the politicians for the parlous state of the Army; though, given that his own views on the shape of war were about as antediluvian as Gilbert's Modern Major-General, he was not entirely blameless for that state. In retirement, he openly attacked the Government's foreign policy, and repeatedly called for a revitalised, strong corporate state; one of his favourite themes being, 'All must join in a *union morale* based on the ideas of Discipline, Patriotism, Duty.'[41] Did Weygand, while in office, go beyond the bounds of propriety in his dealings with the political, as I tried to define them in the first chapter? I think not: indiscreet, perhaps imprudent he may have been in the voicing of his political views, and his association with the right-wing firebrands; but he did not quite cross the frontiers of respectability – not quite and NOT YET. However, to quote the conclusions of an excellent study by Philip Bankwitz, *Maxime Weygand and Civil-Military Relations in Modern France*, Weygand, convinced of the incorrigible anti-military stance of the regime, did employ pressure tactics 'of sufficient intensity and political significance to throw the civil-military relationship into a state of permanent turmoil and to bring it to a point of utter collapse'.[42] Whatever fears might have been generated among the Left, Weygand was never a Boulanger, and – as of the February 1934 crisis – he would have proved a busted flush to any would-be Putschist. Nevertheless, apart from the damage done by Weygand in the other ways which I have described, what was more injurious – and this again comes back to one of the themes outlined in the first chapter – was the mistrust bred from what the good Republicans of the Third Republic feared about Weygand's activities; namely, to have deluded themselves into thinking that the general's bite was worse than his bark.[43]

If Weygand interfered too much in politics, his successor, Maurice Gamelin, went to the opposite extreme of compliant obsequiousness to the State. In a way, the two generals represented the opposite poles of the French Army of the epoch; Weygand, bearing the military's traditional contempt for the politicians; Gamelin, traditional respect for the organs of Government. Having observed at first hand the counter-productive results of his chief's combativeness, Gamelin persuaded himself he could best succeed by operating in 'complete harmony' with the politicians. 'It is by working in all loyalty with the ministers,' he explained in his memoirs,[44] 'and not by sulking that we shall have the right to intervene in debates – otherwise (the command) risks seeing the Government make shift without us.' In March 1936, Gamelin faced his first major test, when Hitler sent his troops into the demilitarised Rhineland. At one stroke France's whole defence strategy lay in ruins. The Maginot Line suddenly became a *cordon sanitaire* protecting Germany, as well as France. Hitler was now free to mop up at will in Eastern Europe; while a frightened Belgium opted out of alliance with France, leaving exposed that fatal open flank north of the Maginot Line. Foch's worst nightmare looked close at hand.

Increasingly, with hindsight, one sees the Rhineland – not Munich two years later – to have been the point at which the Battle in the West was won by Hitler, and lost by France. In March 1936 Gamelin and the French General Staff could – properly – have pressurised the Government to act, on grounds of extreme military necessity. They had the forces, and Hitler would have been compelled to back down – his subsequent career that of General Galtieri. Even if pressure on the Government had failed, then Gamelin could still have fought all-out to woo Soviet military support as a counter-weight in the East. But, true to his philosophy, he remained passive. And passive he was to remain as the slide to war accelerated, through the neglect of the Laval Government, through the industrial disruption and paralysis of the *Front Populaire*, while Hitler rearmed feverishly and French rearmament languished. (During the stewardship of Blum, who had declared 'not a penny, not a man for Berlin' when Hitler marched into the Rhineland, French industrial production in 1938 had sunk an estimated 25 per cent below the 1930 figure; in Germany it had risen 30 per cent.) Under the docile Gamelin (who struck those who met him, like de Gaulle, more as a monkish 'savant'[45] than a fighting soldier), the military and the politicians behaved liked ageing divorcees; reconciled, but not bothering each other. Incredibly, the *Conseil Supérieur de la Guerre* (CSG) met but thirteen times during the four critical years, 1935–9, and was apparently never once consulted about tactical operations of major units. These were the years when the most irreparable damage was done to the French Army (and, incidentally, despite the blame heaped on him subsequently, they were the years when Pétain's influence had been totally removed) – when it was too late for anything like the *Réveil National* of 1911. Gamelin's tragedy was that he was too intelligent to be totally unaware of the dreadful danger.'Fortifications,' he recognised,[46] 'are a means, not an end. The essential instrument of victory is good troops well armed.' But he never pressed this end. Following the occupation of

Czechoslovakia he admitted, that as to a blitzkrieg *attaque brusquée*, 'Until this moment, I remained sceptical; now I believe it could be dangerous.'[47] A masterly understatement – and, of course, it was too late.[48]

On 22 August 1939 Germany and the USSR signed their Non-Aggression Pact, to which Weygand's and Gamelin's policies had placed no obstacle. As Paul Reynaud remarked, 'The Allies had lost the game' – he might have added 'set and match' as well![49] Although nominally at war, for which they were abysmally unprepared, Britain and France sat back and watched while Hitler and Stalin tore Poland apart. For the next eight months of Phoney War they continued to sit like hypnotised rabbits, waiting to be eaten. When the USSR attacked Finland that winter, Weygand was – predictably – writing to Gamelin, 'I regard it as essential to break the back of the Soviet Union in Finland . . . and elsewhere.'[50] The possibility that Britain and France might have had Russia, as well as Germany, on their backs in 1940 makes one's blood run cold; this was only averted by the collapse of brave little Finland.

Meanwhile, whereas – as we have seen – his old master and predecessor, Joffre, in 1914, had set up his GQG out at Chantilly deliberately so as to put himself out of range of interference by the Government, Gamelin set up at Vincennes, on the eastern outskirts of Paris – in order to be as closely in touch with his political masters as possible.[51] This meant, equally, that he was even more out of touch with the front than was Joffre; and his relations with his executive subordinate, General Georges, were appalling. All other comparisons with Joffre are invidious; Gamelin lacked his power, his calm strength of will, his ability – and his forces. On paper, however, those forces were not all that disparate to the Germans'; France in fact had more tanks, and some were better, but they were deployed in an antique fashion throughout the Army, instead of concentrated into powerful *Panzer* divisions.

And of course both she and her British ally were fatally weak in the air. Worst of all, morale was at best patchy. Of his fellow reserve officers, the historian Marc Bloch wrote:

> They received orders from a political system which seemed to them to be corrupted to the very marrow. They were defending a country which they judged in advance to be incapable of resistance. The soldiers whom they commanded issued from the masses which they believed to be degenerate.[52]

Yet, on the other side, by 1940, the *Wehrmacht* – contrary to popularly held beliefs – had not had time to develop into the powerful weapon of standard high quality of either the elder Moltke's army in 1870, or even the younger Moltke's of 1914. It was a bit like a spear with a steel tip and a soft wooden shaft; the tip was formed by the élite *Panzer* and motorised divisions – few in number – while the shaft was made up of the mass of second-rate infantry divisions, often dependent still on horse transport. Had France possessed a concentrated, and determined armoured force capable of slicing into this wooden shaft, who can tell how different the outcome of May 1940 might have been? Finally, however, under Manstein's Plan *Sichelschnitt* the Germans did have the supreme advantage of marching to one of the most outstanding blueprints for victory in the history of war (and which, in part, was replayed by those well-read Israelis in 1973 – with almost equal success).

There is no time here to go into details of the great battle which began when von Rundstedt's forty-five divisions attacked through Belgium and Holland on 10 May 1940. Under the Schlieffen Plan of 1914, the German thrust started in north Belgium, and then wheeled southwards. *Sichelschnitt* in 1940 struck to the south, through the supposedly 'impenetrable' Ardennes, and was to be followed by a hook north-westwards to the Channel ports, ignoring Paris, but encircling the élite of the French and British forces that had moved eastwards to help Belgium. By 13 May, Guderian had broken out across the River Meuse at Sedan, north of where the Maginot Line ended. Two days later, scattering piecemeal French armoured counter-attacks, the *Panzers* had ripped a hole sixty miles wide in the French defences, and were pouring into a bottomless pocket, apparently in the general direction of Paris. That was the day, the sixth day of the campaign, that the battle was in fact lost – as Reynaud (who had succeeded Daladier as Premier in March) admitted in a desperate telephone call to Churchill.

At Vincennes, Gamelin was in an impossible position; he had been under suspended sentence of dismissal ever since the coming-to-power of Reynaud (who contemptuously referred to his generalissimo as 'this nerveless philosopher')[53] he had no *masse de manoeuvre* left; and – this was one of the great beauties of *Sichelschnitt* – he was left in the dark as to whether the *Panzers* were heading for Paris, or for the Channel, until it was far too late. On 20 May, after a series of staggering advances, the Germans reached the Channel, cutting the Allied Armies in two. Meanwhile Reynaud, at last sacking Gamelin, called in the two old soldiers of the First World War – Pétain, aged 84, to be Deputy Premier, and Weygand, 73, who had never held battle command, to succeed Gamelin. Both were committed anti-parliamentarians, and committed defeatists.

Weygand, to his credit, attempted one ill-co-ordinated riposte to slice through the narrow 'Panzer-Corridor'; however, soon on taking up command he made it plain that there could be only 'one last battle', for the sake of the Army's honour, but that France should sue for a separate peace. Already by 25 May, within a week of his arrival, Weygand was characteristically dangling before the Cabinet's eyes the spectre of a Red coup, of a new Commune taking over in Paris; a prospect that seemed to afflict him more than surrender to Hitler. On 12 June he is to be found warning of what happened in Russia in 1917;

and urging (supported by Pétain) that Army divisions be kept intact, 'to maintain order'.

The following day Weygand committed what has been rated as his 'first specific act of disobedience'[54] when he told the Cabinet categorically that he 'would refuse to leave the soil of France even if put in irons'[55] should the Government decide to continue the war in Africa or elsewhere.

The next day, 14 June, the Germans entered Paris. At Bordeaux – housing, once again, as in 1914, the evacuated French Government – Weygand committed a second act of indiscipline by refusing to carry out Premier Reynaud's proposal that France seek a purely military capitulation, leaving her Government – like the Dutch – freedom to continue fighting. He followed this up with a contemptuous aside to a shocked President Lebrun, in which he laid the blame squarely on the politicians. 'For twenty-three years I have followed closely the work of the politicians, ' he declared, 'and I am throroughly aware of all their responsibilities in the current drama.'[56] Here was a clearcut political intervention, and, as Churchill pointed out, Reynaud would have been well within his rights to dismiss his disobedient general. It was a decision, however, that the battered little Premier no longer had either the strength or the will to take. On 16 June he stepped down in favour of Pétain, who, within hours, was approaching the Germans for an armistice; six days later it was signed in the famous railway coach at Réthondes.

Weygand's political role in the armistice of 1940 cannot be overstated. According to one of the Ministers present, Camille Chautemps,[57] it was 'demanded, enforced, imposed' by Weygand on a broken Reynaud. Excusing his breach of discipline, he drew upon a line not dissimilar to that offered up by the Nationalist Generals before the Spanish Civil War; that the 'army was nothing less ... than the Nation,'[58] that it now represented the General Will, which the civil government no longer represented, through having opposed the armistice. On 28 June, he was reinforcing his views, deeply rooted in those experiences of the 1930s, in a memorandum to his new leader, Marshal Pétain: 'The old order of things, that is to say, a political regime of Masonic, capitalist and international compromises, has led us to our present straits. France wants no more of it.'[59]

Weygand's role in June 1940 stands as a major milestone in the history of relations between France's military and the politicians. So too did another act of indiscipline, by a lesser-known French officer, a Brigadier-General Charles de Gaulle, who – on 18 June in London – unfurled the standard of defiance and revolt against Pétain and the armistice. For the next four years the French Army would be split between Vichy and Free France; the consequences, however, of these two interventions on the political scene were to extend far beyond the framework of just the Second World War. Certainly nothing comparable had happened to the French Army previously during this century under review.[60]

IV

The Savage Wars of Peace, 1945–70

'Take up the White Man's Burden –
The savage wars of peace –
Fill full the mouth of famine
And bid the sickness cease.'

Rudyard Kipling

We ended the last chapter at perhaps the darkest moment in the long history of the French Army. In France, 84-year-old Marshal Pétain, the hero of Verdun, had accepted an armistice from Hitler, on the most humiliating terms; in England, disobeying all orders to return to France, a lanky 49-year-old brigadier had, with two or three thousand men, set up the Cross of Lorraine – an act of indiscipline for which he was condemned to death *in absentia*. As the French historian, Paul-Marie de la Gorce, remarks, ' For the French Army, the age of the individual began on June 18, 1940. A full twenty years later, it had not yet ended.'[1] On the *Quatorze Juillet* the traditional military parade took place, at Vichy, with Pétain taking the salute of a few hundred forlorn troops of 'miserable appearance', so Paul Baudouin described them. It was in

67

bitter contrast to the splendour of the first *Quatorze* of sixty years previously, and of all those that had succeeded. Little more impressive – though undoubtedly showing better spirit – was the performance put on simultaneously in Britain by de Gaulle's handful of followers.

The outstanding significance of the two ceremonies was that they stamped the seal on the fact that, the civil government of the Third Republic having failed, and abdicated its powers, for the next four war years France would be split between two governments – and each of them headed by a soldier.[2] Here we come face to face with the terrible problem of conflicting loyalties, and the whole issue of legitimacy – which had not raised its head, certainly with such grave consequences, since 1870–1. What this meant to the conscience of the average French soldier between 1940 and the Liberation has perhaps not been better stated than by General Eisenhower in his *Crusade in Europe*:

> It is possible to understand why de Gaulle was disliked within the ranks of the French Army. At the time of France's surrender in 1940, the officers who remained in the Army had accepted the position and the orders of their government and had given up the fight. In their view, if the course chosen by de Gaulle was correct, then every French officer who obeyed the orders of his government was a poltroon. If de Gaulle was a loyal Frenchman they had to regard themselves as cowards. Naturally the officers did not choose to think of themselves in this light; rather they considered themselves as loyal Frenchmen carrying out the orders of constituted civilian authority.[3]

Thus both camps had good reason for feeling that they were doing the patriotic thing. It was an agonising dilemma, one which Anglo-Saxon armies have fortunately been spared, so far – since Cromwell, or the US Civil War. (As indication of the dimensions of the *crise de conscience*, one may note in passing that one small group of French officers, and several from the old nobility, who were unable to accept the legitimacy of either Pétain or de Gaulle, took themselves to the Soviet Union, where they formed the 'Normandie-Niemen Air Squadron', which fought with utmost courage and dreadful losses on the Russian front for the rest of the war.)[4]

Whatever one may feel about Pétain and Vichy – and, indeed, Weygand – one must take note of a most important fact, perhaps insufficiently recognised heretofore; namely, the quite remarkable way in which the French Army was both reconstituted, and the mainstream of its traditions kept alive, following the Armistice. Pétain once even went so far as to declare forthrightly to Hitler: 'You judge rightly that a State cannot long endure without a disciplined army. I have as my first duty to reconstitute an army capable of assuring the security of France and of her Empire.'[5]

Here justice must be paid, too, to the role of Weygand – and equally also to his success in keeping the Germans out of French North Africa, where the 120,000-strong core of the new 'Armistice Army' was safely kept: although Weygand was to become one of the principal post-liberation whipping-boys of the Gaullists.[6] Once again, rather as General Trochu and the post-1870 regime had done, Vichy and its Army started the resurrection from the premise that the recent débâcle had been caused by defaults more on the spiritual than the military level. In training, a certain boy-scoutism was prevalent, with great emphasis on moral – and political – 're-education', on parades and what the British Brigade of Guards would call 'swank'. No officer entered into all this with more enthusiasm than Weygand's former contact-man with the right-wing groupings, de Lattre de Tassigny, now a general whose division had been one of the few to acquit itself with distinction in May 1940. Difficult as it was to conceal activities, and weapons, from the German inspection teams, the Army was helped by its withdrawal within itself (for certain understandable psychological reasons), and isolation from the civilian world more marked than at any other period since 1870. With a soldier – and the hero of Verdun – at the head of state for the first time since MacMahon, many officers felt their interests well looked after, the despised politicians of the Third Republic properly relegated to the dustbin of history. It is noteworthy that, after the summer of 1940, relatively few regular officers left to join the Gaullists; who, even after the Allied invasion of North Africa, remained a small group in relation to the Vichy Army, in numbers as well as outlook. Following the British and Free French seizure of Syria in 1941, for instance, less than one-in-six of the Vichy troops there opted to joined de Gaulle.

After April 1942, however, when Laval took over the reins, there was a new interference in the Army by the political; with a resulting debasement in morale. Meanwhile the Resistance had begun to make headway in the Unoccupied Zone; yet – equally – few regular officers took to the hills with it, partly because of its unprofessionalism, but mostly because of its strong Communist orientations. Here again one finds echoes of the Weygand era of the 1930s; the predominant, ugly fear that joining in common cause with the Left in the Underground would inevitably lead, eventually, to a Communist take-over. (It is interesting to recall that during the drive on Paris in 1944 de Gaulle too was to exhort General Leclerc 'Go fast; we cannot have another Commune.')[7]

Then, in November 1942, Eisenhower's British and Americans landed in North Africa. The defending Vichy troops there faced another dilemma of 'excruciating complexity': 'They might obey standing orders to resist any and all invaders; they might do nothing until clearer orders from higher authority had been received; or they might issue orders on their own authority contrary to standing orders to resist.'[8] Here is the typical reaction of one junior officer:

I stopped believing in the virtue of obedience the day when, on a Moroccan beach, I received two contradictory orders at ten minutes' interval; one from my major, to rally with my section to the disembarking American troops; the other from my colonel, to resist to the bitter end.[9]

Just twenty years later, it would not be far from those Moroccan beaches – in Algeria – that French officers would contemplate the virtues of disobedience, this time towards President de Gaulle, more weightily than at any other time in French history. Meanwhile, in 1942 many died in what they held to be their duty to the nation, as represented then by the person of Marshal Pétain. On 11 November, the Germans crossed into Unoccupied France. Only one senior commander, disobeying Vichy instructions to stay in barracks, attempted – unsuccessfully – to resist. Escaping a ten-year prison sentence for indiscipline, de Lattre de Tassigny fled to join the French forces in North Africa, thence to become France's top soldier at the Liberation. The Armistice Army now ceased to exist with the German invasion of Vichy France, and the French Army of the future had its being almost entirely in North Africa – of which the Gaullist contingent numbered only little more than 10 per cent. This was a fact of life that was to have considerable bearing on the course of events in Algeria a decade and a half later.[10]

After the Liberation, there was contemptuous talk in the Army about the *napthalinards* – those Armistice Army officers who had taken their uniforms out of mothballs just in time for the celebration parades. Nevertheless, it was no accident that the Vichy Armistice Army provided France's top post-war general, de Lattre; for it also provided the nucleus of the Army of the new Fourth Republic, bringing with it its own attitudes of mind, superimposed on the traditions of the old pre-1940 Army. It is noteworthy that many of the officers who had served in the ARO, the Army Resistance Organisation created in Unoccupied France, found themselves on the excluded list, along with those tainted with 'collaboration'. Of one sample of 970 Resistance leaders commissioned in July 1945, only 187 subsequently received regular commissions. A considerable number of the Free French, who had 'broken discipline' between June 1940 and November 1942, were themselves shunted off to dim staff jobs, rather than active commands. Among them were General Koenig, hero of Bir Hakim, and General Billotte, who had escaped from a prison camp in Russia to become de Gaulle's right-hand man, and was retired at forty-four in 1950. On the other hand, de Lattre and Juin, high officers under Vichy, became marshals (the latter, the last to survive – perhaps the last ever?). Among the young, early Gaullist officers to pursue a successful regular career, was a rugged young man called Jacques Massu who had entered Paris with Leclerc's famous Second Armoured Division: having broken discipline once, Massu is described by Robert Paxton in his excellent study, *Parades and Politics at Vichy*,[11] as becoming later 'the very prototype of the factious general'.[12] (Of de Gaulle himself, Paxton remarks that, according to the Armistice Army's standards of discipline, he was 'the most conspicuous example of the insubordinate officer whose bad example was abundantly rewarded.')[12] Other officers to find themselves in the same camp with Massu in Algeria, the Generals Challe and Salan, had – on the contrary – both served under Pétain. There was much arbitrary unfairness in the choice of who should be offered a career in the post-Liberation Army, and who rejected. Said Admiral Abrial, bitterly, at his trial:

> I nearly became maritime prefect of Algiers, instead of taking my job as maritime prefect of Toulon. If that had happened, I would be Minister of the Navy today instead of being in Fresnes Prison... simple geography had a lot to do with it.[13]

All the rancour and divisions that swept over France in the aftermath of war pervaded the Army too, causing new chasms within it, as well as a fresh sense of isolation from the Nation – both important factors in all that was to follow.[14]

Among the distinguished Gaullists to hold a high post after 1945 was General Leclerc, leader of the famous march from Lake Chad in the early days of the Free French; a Jesuit-trained aristocrat and St Cyrien, who was sent to Indo-China in 1945 to restore the French presence there. (Tragically killed in an aircrash in 1947, he was posthumously created *Maréchal de France.*) From here began what soon came to be known as France's *sale guerre* – and which, of course, led in a direct line to America's long involvement in Vietnam. For France it was to mean that, between 1939 and 1962, the French Army would enjoy no more than a few weeks of true peace. In the eight years that it dragged on, the running sore of the Indo-China War cost France more than the total she received in Marshall Aid, an annual 10 per cent of the national budget; was to swallow up an entire class of St Cyr officers every three years; and to account – by the time it ended at Dien Bien Phu – for 75 000 French casualties in dead and missing alone. As Raymond Aron noted: 'In order to maintain herself in Indo-China, France committed more military strength than had been needed to establish herself there.'[15] The same could be said later with equal truth of Algeria. France, uniquely among the Western powers, chose – or was forced – to expand rather than reduce the size of her army in the immediate post-war years. From 1945 to 1947, the global size of the French military establishment (all services) fell rapidly from 1.2 million to 490 000; but from there it rose steadily back to the 1.2 million figure by 1957. The expense involved was one that a war-weary and economically rickety France could ill-afford: which made the *sale guerre* progressively more unpopular.

It has been suggested often enough that, had the French military government in Indo-China, and its political masters in Paris, only put out a friendly hand to Ho Chi Minh in the early days, a *combinazione* might have been arrived at. So be it; this is not the place to explore the origins of that war. Enough to say that, for different motives, both the politicians and the military found themselves inextricably committed to the *sale guerre*. De Gaulle[16] said of this that 'the determination to win the war had alternated with the desire to make peace without anyone being able to decide between the two'.[17]

Whatever the motives of the politicians in hanging on to Indo-China, the Army discovered a special mission for itself there. Alsace-Lorraine had long been restored, Hitler was destroyed and Germany flattened, and the European Defence Community was neither a popular, nor a romantic conception. The enemy (partly a hangover from Vichy and pre-1939 traditions, but also suddenly become infinitely – and genuinely – more menacing) was now Soviet Communism; but where, to the élite paras engaged in the war, it most directly confronted the West was in the jungles and paddy fields of Indo-China. Gradually they came to convince themselves that they were defending a bastion of Western civilisation against Communism. There was also an element of *la Gloire* involved as François Mitterrand wrote in 1957, 'When the war in Indo-China broke out, France was able to believe that the 1940 defeat was nothing more than a lost battle, and that the armistice of 1945 was going to restore its power at the same time as its glory.'[18]

Then, once again, soldiering in France had become unattractive. Between 1945 and 1950 in terms of comparative salary rating, a colonel had fallen from third to ninth place (and to thirteenth by 1960). By 1960, too, a customs collector would have comfortably outstripped the earnings of an army major. As of 1953, the same major would have received only two-thirds of what his British equivalent could expect, and one-third of his American equivalent. And so, *pari passu*, did prestige slump. The story was not dissimilar to what we have seen in those other days when the French populace felt it no longer needed men-in-arms – after the 1880s and post-1918. As the *sale guerre* dragged on, apparently unwinnable, the French nation seemed to want to know less and less about its Army. By May 1953, 65 per cent of a poll declared for ending the war: but still the politicians ordered its soldiers to go on fighting. On the other side, a sense of alienation from *la Nation* grew among the troops: 'You don't know these people,' wrote an officer of the colonial parachutists,[19] closely echoing what Barbusse's famous novel, *Le Feu*,[20] had to say about the 'two fronts' in the First World War, 'You have nothing to do with them (the metropolitan bourgeois), it's another universe.'[21] In retrospect, he no longer thought of his 'period in Indo-China', but of his 'period in France': 'Things made more sense in the war, there he felt at home, and elsewhere he was abroad.' Pay was also better in Indo-China; ditto, later, in Algeria. Following a direct line from the 1930s, Weygand, and the Vichy Army, the officers of Indo-China blamed the politicians for all that went wrong in this particularly unpleasant *sale guerre* of ambushes by unseen guerrillas. 'Now we know that a French Army, on no matter what territory it fights, will always be stabbed in the back,' wrote one veteran with characteristic bitterness.[22]

When General Leclerc opened up talks with the Vietminh back in 1945, the Army in Indo-China inevitably became embroiled in politics; it was not to extricate itself – or, rather, be extricated – until the end of the Algerian War in 1962. Significantly it was Leclerc's chief negotiator in 1945, a General Raoul Salan, who was to leak to the press a report on the war (by General Ely) highly embarrassing to the civil French Government, and who in the Algerian War would take even more dramatically direct action against the Government. The demands of guerrilla warfare also imposed solutions that were no longer purely military. Colonel Lacheroy, one of the new breed of 'thinking' colonels to emerge from Indo-China, wrote: 'The norms we used to estimate the opposing forces, the traditional norms, are dead. We have to examine a form of warfare that is new in its conceptions and new in its practices. This is the form of warfare we call "revolutionary war".'[23] Another philosopher/soldier of importance, General Lionel-Martin Chassin, wrote (in 1954),[24]

It is time for the Army to cease being the *grande muette* ... What can the Western nations do to avoid the accomplishment of Mao's plan for world conquest? We must oppose a struggle based on subversion with the same weapons, oppose faith with faith, propaganda with propaganda, and an insidious and powerful ideology with a superior one capable of winning the hearts of men.

and, recalling the decay of the Eastern Roman Empire,[25]

Whatever the extent of disorder and internal anarchy, all can be saved so long as one disposes of a solid and sufficiently national army capable of fulfilling two historical functions in a period of disintegration; defend the empire without and place in power within a leader capable of effecting the necessary rectification in re-establishing order and authority.

Heady stuff. Urging the Army to involve itself to an increasing degree in politics, Chassin and his psy-warfare colleagues expounded the view that proper indoctrination of the French nation was as important as indoctrinating colonial populations.

If they despised the politicians, the young 'revolutionary' colonels also had little higher opinion of their old school generals.[26] Perhaps rightly. At the end of 1953, the French High Command planted its main striking force in an isolated, Verdun-like position called Dien Bien Phu. General Giap took up the gauntlet, and after a fifty-six-day siege that cost the French defenders 13 000 lives, Dien Bien Phu surrendered in May 1954. In June the Laniel

Government was replaced by Mendès-France, who promised he would have France out of the *sale guerre* in thirty-three days. He was as good as his word. But the French Army left Indo-China with a bad conscience gnawing at them over what they considered a base betrayal of the Catholic population there. If the *sale guerre* had turned its French Army pupils into superb warriors, it had, however, also made them highly political animals. And the peace, the first since September 1939, was to last just three months and four days.

In his book, *Inside Africa*, published in 1955, John Gunther noted as a postscript[27] that on 1 November 1954, All Saints Day, 'a small but serious armed rebellion broke out against the French authorities in eastern Algeria, much to the chagrin of Paris ... after a week the rebels were put down and order restored'. This was not quite how history turned out; the second *sale guerre*, in Algeria, was to continue for nearly another eight years, almost twice as long as the First World War, and was to bring France herself to the brink of civil war. In its way it provides a kind of climax towards which these lectures have been stumbling.

The Algerian War is a vastly complex affair; there were, in effect, at least seven separate wars, revolutions or struggles, all going on upon different planes at the same time. First there was

- The fighting war itself
- The political war for the 'middle-ground' in Algeria
- A civil war between Algerians
- A revolutionary struggle within the leadership of the Algerian FLN (*Front de Libération Nationale*)
- The external war fought on the platforms of the outside world (which, as per Vietnam, was perhaps the most decisive)
- A struggle between the *Pied Noir* settlers of Algeria,

and France, culminating in open warfare under the aegis of the OAS (*Organisation Armée Secrète*)

and, finally, and which interests us here most

● A struggle between the French Army in Algeria and the Government in Paris, leading in the first place to the overthrow of the Fourth Republic, and the advent of de Gaulle, and later to a full-scale revolt against de Gaulle himself

France's involvement in Algeria harks back to 1830; but why, one might ask, did she hang on to it so desperately after 1954, when Mendès-France was ready to give up Indo-China, Tunisia and Morocco? The answer is, primarily, that, in 1848, the fateful step was taken of declaring it – unique among all other French possessions – an integral part of France. Thus every successive government was lumbered with the albatross round its neck of Algeria being, not a colony, but an inseparable part of France herself – like Languedoc or the Dordogne. Thus when the revolt began in 1954, Mendès-France declared, '*Ici, c'est la France!*', while his Minister of the Interior, a good Socialist called François Mitterrand took an even more hawkish line: 'The only possible declaration is war ... for Algeria is France.'[28] However, a secondary answer to why France hung on to Algeria may be sought for in the fact that the French Army was to make a troth out of *Algérie Française*.

The numerous contributory causes of the FLN revolt can only be dealt with in outline here, but they will not be altogether unfamiliar to anyone who has studied southern Africa recently; predominantly, a minority of approximately one million Europeans, nicknamed *Pieds Noirs* – perhaps because metropolitan Frenchmen scornfully considered their feet to have been burned black by too much sun – who were surrounded by a sea of nine million indigenous Moslem Algerians. Demographically, the

Algerian birthrate was exploding; economically, the gulf between Algerian and *Pied Noir* expectations was widening. Politically, the Algerians had little more real power than the Rhodesian blacks under Ian Smith.

During the first two years, the war looked unwinnable by either side. The FLN had inadequate equipment to fight more than a series of guerilla actions; the French had not enough troops to be everywhere in this vast territory, now the world's tenth largest nation in area. So in 1956, Guy Mollet, another French Socialist, took the dramatic step of first sending half a million conscripts to Algeria. The most notable effect this had was to spread awareness about the war to metropolitan France; much as the escalation of the USA's commitment in Vietnam did in America. Meanwhile the FLN, with consummate skill in canvassing support within the Afro-Asian Third World, in the US and at the UN, had gone far to internationalise what France determinedly maintained was a private, internal dispute.

In the autumn of 1956, coincidental with the disastrous Suez operation, by a daring *coup-de-main* in mid air, of highly dubious legality, and without the sanction of the French Government, French army intelligence hijacked Ben Bella and the entire external leadership of the FLN. Here was surely an instance of improper military intervention on the political level – and the impropriety was to multiply. In 1957, through resorting to the toughest measures (about which, more later), General Massu's élite paras won what looked like a clear-cut military victory in the famous 'Battle of Algiers', breaking up the whole FLN network in the city. But in April 1958, after one economic crisis after another, Premier Gaillard fell, leaving France without a government in the most dangerous power vacuum since 1945. The war had already toppled five governments, and was about to bring down the Fourth Republic itself. In May the FLN executed three French soldiers; this was the last straw for the hard-tried French Army in

Algeria. As de Gaulle says of it: 'Taking upon itself not only the burden of fighting, but also the severity, and sometimes the beastliness, of the repression ... haunted by fear of another Indo-China ... the army, more than any other body, felt a growing resentment against a political system which was the embodiment of irresolution.'[29]

On 13 May, after emotional scenes in Algiers, preceded by weeks of conspiracy and counter-conspiracy, an army-controlled Committee of Public Safety took over in Algiers, under the leadership of the C-in-C – General Raoul Salan. It was the first time since June 1940 that the French military had intervened directly in national politics. Explaining the action in a telephone call to Paris, Massu[30] declared, 'There is no question of a *coup d'état* ... It's just to confirm to parliament the will of Algeria to remain French.' Rousseau's 'General Will' was being invoked (just as de Gaulle and Weygand had, separately, invoked it in 1940) and in the ensuing threats by the paras to drop on France there was a further alarming similarity with the scenario that preceded the Spanish Civil War. Called for by the Algiers generals, de Gaulle averted the first of three possible threats of civil war that were to occur over as many years by agreeing to form a government – but on his terms. The Fifth Republic had begun.

De Gaulle, however, then allowed valuable months to pass without producing any new solution for Algeria. The Army soon began to distrust their man, as speaking with too many voices; one French observer (in 1960) said he was like Molière's Don Juan who had 'promised marriages to five or six women and absolutely had to avoid being pinned down by any of them!'[31] Whereas, to the French Army and the *Pieds Noirs*, Algeria was everything, to de Gaulle it was only one factor in his overall ambition: the resurrection of the greater glory of France – and it was on no account to get in the way of that. In September 1959, de Gaulle offered the Algerians the fateful words of 'self-determination'. Three months later, following on de Gaulle's sacking of the popular General Massu, Algiers boiled over. There was a shoot-up in which fourteen French gendarmes were killed, and for a week extremist *Pieds Noirs* dug themselves in behind barricades. What was worse, some of the élite para units showed signs of fraternising with the *Pieds Noirs* behind the barricades. For the second time, it looked as if France might be facing civil war. Like Thiers during the Commune of 1871, de Gaulle now realised how brittle an instrument the Army was. By June 1960 he had decided he had to negotiate with the FLN; because of the FLN's obduracy, however, negotiations were to spin out over almost another two years.

Then, on 21 April 1961, four senior generals of the Army of Algeria revolted and seized power in Algiers. One of the rebel generals was Salan, formerly of Indo-China, the C-in-C who had first opened the door to de Gaulle in May 1958; but of far weightier consequence was the leader of the 'Generals' Putsch' – Maurice Challe.

Challe was one of the most esteemed and honourable officers in the French Army – or, for that matter, any army. As an airman, he seemed the embodiment of the ideal Republican general, leaning if anything towards the Socialists. He had come closer than any other C-in-C to winning the war on the ground; but in doing so he felt that he had – in the name of de Gaulle – traduced undertakings to the loyal Muslim levies, called *Harkis,* that France would never abandon them. Honour left him no alternative but revolt. (Meanwhile two other top generals, Ely and Valluy had quietly resigned. Like Challe and Salan both had been in the Vichy Army; Ely, who had served in both World Wars, was haunted by fears of a new split in the Army along the lines of 1940.) Poorly prepared, the Algiers revolt lasted four days; but during that time France edged closer to the brink of civil war than ever before. Once again, a superbly timed broadcast by de

Gaulle, in which he showed transcending command over public opinion, won the day. In the mass, the servicemen, and particularly the conscripts, heeded the President rather than their rebel officers, in what became known as the 'Battle of the Transistors'. Many officers also suddenly realised that the Army and the Nation had reached a parting of the ways, and civil war was a frontier they were not prepared to risk crossing.[32]

Nevertheless, some 14 000 officers and men had been implicated in the revolt, and the French Army was badly split – with effects that were to last long beyond the Algerian War. Many of its finest officers had their careers ruined. Challe, expecting the death sentence, spent many years in prison. His was a personal tragedy that should perhaps be pondered by all other Western leaders, should they ever come to impose too great a burden upon the consciences of their generals. Meanwhile, de Gaulle's bargaining hand was gravely weakened by the revolt, followed by the mounting atrocities committed by the underground OAS – which was headed by a fugitive General Salan – and he now had to negotiate from a position of total weakness. On 18 March 1962, a ceasefire was signed.

A few extra words need to be said about the nature of the French Army in Algeria. As *Le Monde* once stated, few other forces possessed a generation of officers who had fought so much; and, since 1940, most of their battles had ended in humiliation – which they ascribed more to the deviousness and incompetence of the politicians than to any martial failings on their part. They became deeply attached to the soil of Algeria; life there was a good one, and economically attractive. The units arriving from Indo-China represented perhaps the toughest and most efficient fighting force in the world at that date. Victories like the 'Battle of Algiers' convinced them that they *could* win the war – and, for deep psychological reasons based on those defeats of the past, it was a war they *had* to win.

These tough regulars were, above all, men with a mission: 'We want to halt the decadence of the West and the march of Communism. That is our duty, the real duty of the army. That is why we must win the war in Algeria. Indo-China taught us to see the truth,'[33] declared Colonel Antoine Argoud, an old Indo-China hand who later typified the ringleaders in the 'Generals' Putsch' against de Gaulle in 1961, and later still was one of the fallen angels of the OAS.

The question was, were they fighting the right war? As noted earlier, the paras came from Indo-China thoroughly steeped in the doctrines of Mao and General Giap, and they put these to good use in the methods of psychological and political warfare they introduced into Algeria. To combat FLN agitation and propaganda in the field, and to maintain the *présence française* there, a system called the SAS, *Sections Administratives Spéciales*, was instituted. Each of some 400 was usually run by a dedicated, and extremely brave young captain, who would live among the rural Algerians as a combined mayor, judge and welfare officer. It was not unlike the colonial army in the days of Lyautey and Mangin. Unfortunately, there were never enough of the good SAS officers to go round, and they were prime targets for the FLN terrorists (And, of course, this all meant a further political involvement for the Army.) It should be said here that, for all the allegations of brutality, many of the French army officers in the field had the most altruistic motives towards the Algerians, and were genuine liberals in the sense that they saw nothing in common with the rich *colons* who exploited the Muslims.

It must also be noted, however, that to some extent the psy-war experts seemed to be fighting the wrong enemy. (They often even referred to the FLN as 'Viets'.) For, although Ho and Giap and the whole Vietminh set-up had been thoroughly steeped in Marxist doctrine from the earliest days, Communism had minimal influence over the FLN; which was, essentially, a nationalist movement.

In fact, the French Communist Party often ranged itself on the other side. Nevertheless, the Army tended to see the war in terms of an international conspiracy of the Left. Pleading for his life at his trial in 1962, Salan represented the views of many officers when he declared, 'I do not have to exonerate myself for having refused to allow Communism to be established an hour away from Marseilles.'[34] Again, one detects the legacy of the 1930s – and, indeed, of the Commune.[35]

In 1957, when the French gendarmerie showed itself incapable of mastering terrorism in Algiers, Governor-General Lacoste had called in General Massu and his paras. This was a most fateful step; it meant that the Army, especially the paras – following General Chassin's advice – would be most closely involved in political matters, from which henceforward they would never quite divorce themselves. At the Barricades Trial, Colonel Broizat of the paras explained: 'If we ... became interested in the political problem, it was not because of a taste for politicking; it was because of the demands of our professional duty.'[36] From 1958 onwards, the paras grew increasingly into an élite among the army in Algeria. 'There is a tiny percentage who really attack, and the others. The paras attack.'

Tactically, this made it more difficult for the High Command to deploy troops of equal quality; and, because of the paras' political involvement, it also meant that no government of the Fourth Republic, no matter how vigorous (which none were) would be able to abandon *Algérie française* without serious obstruction from the para-led army. From here a direct line led to the Army *coup* of May 1958, and finally to the *putsch des généraux* of April 1961.

We now come to the ugly issue of torture. Acting with great speed and ruthlessness, Massu's action in Algiers in 1957 registered high success; by the end of the year, the FLN had to admit to its first big *military* defeat of the war. I stress the word *military*. For the 'Battle of Algiers' could

probably not have been won without resort to in-
stitutionalised torture – freely admitted by Massu – on a
large scale. The long-term result of this was that, although
it may have won the battle, it lost the war for France
through the violent and persistent reaction which it
aroused both in the mother country and the world at
large.

Therein lies a grave warning for any country which
might be tempted to employ torture as an instrument of
policy; it is always a dangerously double-edged, self-
destructive weapon. As one distinguished French soldier,
General Pierre Billotte, remarked of it in Algeria:[37] 'Whatever its form and whatever its purpose, it is unacceptable,
inadmissible, condemnable; it soils the honour of the
army and the country.'[38]

Finally, one arrives at the differences between the
politician and the military, and the limitations of the latter
– in so far as they concern the course of the war in Algeria:
'The one, who sees dimly from afar, judges realities to be
complex and applies himself to grasp them by ruse and
calculation; the other, who sees clearly but from close up,
finds them to be simple and believes that one dominates
them if only one is resolved to do so.'[39] By the beginning of
1960, General Challe – then C-in-C in Algeria – with his
new offensive techniques had certainly come close to
defeating the FLN militarily. But, what Challe, with the
clear, though blinkered vision of the soldier, could not see
was that – although the fighting war was virtually won on
the ground – it had also been lost on the diplomatic and
political fronts of the outside world; including within
France herself. It is useful to note here, as a kind of
preview of the US experience in Vietnam, the intense
barrage of anti-war propaganda from France to which the
Army in Algeria was subjected – particularly from 1960
onwards, playing a conspicuous role in the failure of the
Putsch des Généraux in April 1961. There was the 'Manifesto
of the 121', organised by Simone de Beauvoir and others of

the Left, which openly incited conscripts to desert. There was the 'letter to soldiers' from the OCC (*Organisation civile du contingent*), backed – unofficially – by the Socialists; and there was the more militant CAC (*Comité d'action au sein du contingent*), which reached soldiers on leave with roneo'd sheets, warning them against what they might be called upon to do contrary to the 'honour of the Republic'.[40]

Here, then, was one of the most important consequences of the Algerian War on the politico-military plane; because of the interplay of modern communications with the presence of vast numbers of civilian conscripts on active duty, the Army – try as it might – could no longer see itself as standing aloof, separated and isolated, as it had once done, from *La Nation.*

So ends the Algerian War; the longest, and gravest crisis the French Army has ever had to face. On the French side, the last and perhaps saddest act in the tragedy was the trial of the distinguished officers who had revolted against de Gaulle and the established civil government of France. At Salan's trial, the veteran anti-Gaullist lawyer, Mâitre Tixier-Vignancourt, made an eloquent – and successful, in that he saved Salan's life – plea to the court[41] that, since 18 June 1940 – when de Gaulle himself raised the standard of revolt in London – all French officers had 'learned the wisdom of disobeying orders which violated the promptings of conscience'. Or, as Colonel Argoud had phrased a similar plea at the Barricades Trial of 1960, 'On a certain day in June 1940, officers of France were called upon to choose between the way of honour and that of discipline. Some chose honour; much more numerous, discipline. One cannot say precisely that all were rewarded for their decision.'[42] Here was, indeed, a *tu quoque* argument of undeniable force; and, while it is dangerous to draw too sweeping conclusions, it is significant that most of the leading anti-Gaullist rebels of 1961 – such as Challe and Salan – were those who obeyed Pétain in 1940. As Robert Paxton notes, 'Wartime memories were more likely to make dissidents out of the obedient officers of 1940 and vice versa . . . the breach was all the more irreparable because the Armistice Army had done nothing to bridge the ancient gap between professional officers and French civilian society.'[43]

One is inevitably reminded of the much-quoted speech by Ulysses, made in another military context:

> '. . . untune that string,
> And, hark! what discord follows. . . .'

And, indeed, the whole drama of the continuum of struggles between the French Army and the body politic from 1870 to 1940, followed by the 'discord' between 1940 and 1962, then the pursuit of equilibrium restored after 1962 to our present day, does bring to mind parallels with those History Plays of Shakespeare.[44]

I began by saying that certain themes would repeat themselves throughout this book; one might perhaps try to synthesise them under four broad headings:

- The *armée de metier* versus the conscript army, heir to the *levée en masse.*
- The Army's place in society; separate or integrated? (and under this I would include such matters as social structure and conditions of service).
- The role of the Army; how much was it the guardian of *internal*, as well as external security?

and leading on from here.

- The issue of the Army's loyalty, and its assessment of the 'legitimacy' of the regime it served – never more under stress than during the Algerian War.

Once Algeria was out of the way, de Gaulle's main concern was the total restructuring of the French Army. It was somehow symbolic that France's first atomic bomb should have been detonated at Reggane in the Algerian Sahara just two weeks after the Barricades revolt, while a further bomb exploded as the 1961 *Putsch* was collapsing. One of de Gaulle's principal motives in wanting to disentangle the Army from Algeria was to modernise it, to transform it into an up-dated version of his 1930s dream of the *armée de métier*, of which the atomic *Force de Frappe* was an essential component. 'You don't take Algeria away from the Army and then bring them home to shoot popguns!', remarks Harvard's Professor Stanley Hoffmann,[45] and – although there followed some bitter infighting as to which of the three services was to be its ultimate beneficiary – France's new atomic age Army undoubtedly did bear with it a vital sop for the loss of Algeria. The Army cadres also accepted that the projected role of the *Force de Frappe* should be primarily one of political prestige, rather than as a purely military accessory, at the same time as, by and large, they supported de Gaulle's withdrawal from NATO for the military independence, and extra authority, it granted them. (The associated principle of '*Tous Azimuts*'[46] was also not unpopular – given the Vichy influences which lasted into the 1960s, with the bitter memories of the sinking of the French Fleet at Mers-el-Kebir in 1940, and other subsequent humiliations at the hands of the Anglo-Saxon allies.)[47]

After 1962, however, the officer corps was extensively reshaped. The élite para and Foreign Legion regiments deeply implicated in the 1961 Putsch were broken up, their officers either purged or forced out in droves by such indirect pressures as ostentatious surveillance, frequent changes of post, forced separation from families, and passed-over promotions. Already in Indo-China and Algeria there had been an increased democratisation through promotions from the ranks, and a falling-off in the intake of the old-school St Cyrien nobility, and these trends continued. The Army remained conservative, though perhaps slightly less so than before, and more bourgeois than aristocratic in its composition compared with the past.

The late sixties and early seventies were a period of unrest and tension within the French forces. Decolonialisation and adjustment to the changes wrought by nuclear weaponry were part of the root cause; but perhaps more immediate was the discontent of French youth with the terms, and conditions, of national service. The Giscard Government tried to tackle this last problem by appointing the legendary para hero of the Algerian War, General Marcel Bigeard, to be State Secretary to the Ministry of Defence with the duty of 'remoralising' the army, and ridding it of revolutionary elements. As so often when front-line soldiers are brought into politics, the appointment was not a success; however, with the passage of time and modernising of some aspects of military life, discontent waned. Then, as the old Algeria hands gradually disappeared, so much of the bitterness and frustration was drained away too, and by the 1970s there had arisen a new, streamlined and highly professional Army, with a global total of little over half a million, and with better pay and conditions than heretofore, based entirely on French soil and with a simplified new mission – to defend France.[48]

With the passage of time, and the coming of Mitterrand, one detects a curious swing in traditional attitudes towards conscription. On the one hand, in a poll of 1973, some 72 per cent of all officers favoured conscription (set at twelve months under the laws of 1970 and 1971), while Alexandre Sanguinetti, the former Gaullist Minister, dropped a bombshell by declaring that six months was long enough; on the other hand, Charles Hernu, the Socialist expert on defence and later Minister, agreed with a reduction to six months, and once even suggested that the Holy Grail of conscription might eventually be abandoned altogether. (As has often happened when Socialists brought to power in Britain have proved to be well-disposed to Army wishes, in the event Hernu acceded to the Army's desire for twelve months, on grounds of practicality.) At the same time Mitterrand and Hernu have also accepted unequivocally the nuclear *Force de Frappe*, much attacked by the Left previously when out of power. (In noting the contrast in protests against nuclear weaponry inside France compared with, for instance, Britain and West Germany in the early 1980s it has been suggested that an explanation could be found in the fact that, under the independent *Force de Frappe*, France has her own 'finger on the button' and not that of the US High Command).[49]

Prior to the 1974 presidential elections which brought the first prospect of a Socialist/Communist dominated government, there were rumbles of '*l'Armée bouge*'. But, in fact, when Mitterrand did come to power in 1981, neither did the Army 'move', nor were there even any notable number of officer resignations. Of course, one cannot predict – any more than with contemporary Spain – how the French Army might react, were there to be a serious threat of the Communists grasping the reins; or even if there were to occur a major economic crisis that seriously impaired the funding of the Armed Forces. Yet, as of the date of writing, for the time being there seems to have been achieved a truce – even if finely balanced, something that is rare in the history of French politico-military relations that we have been tracing. On the one hand, we have the Mitterrand Socialists making it clear that they would not tolerate the use of the Army for quelling domestic or industrial disorders (as Charles Hernu puts it in his book, *Soldat-Citoyen*, 'The army cannot be placed in the service of a minority in order to repress a majority'.[50]); on the other hand, undertaking to eschew any attempts to carry trades union activities, or 'socialisation', into its ranks. Both sides seem to have accepted the other's position; with the Socialists, in effect, making the quite remarkable concession that the Army does have a separate identity of its own – or what, in current government jargon, is called 'specificity' – within *La Nation*. Almost as a seal of this compact is the fact that the new French Chief of Defence Forces (CEMA), General Lacaze, should be – for the first time since the Algerian War – an officer who served in Algeria with one of the stigmatised para regiments; truly a sign of 'all is forgiven'.[51]

After the Mitterrand Socialists came to power through free elections, under rules established by de Gaulle, there took place a kind of honeymoon in which the whole bitter question of army loyalty, and the associated issue of legitimacy, *looked* more settled than for many a decade. Nevertheless, as this book goes to press, France has been shaken by the resignation of the Chief of the Army Staff, General Delaunay, apparently as a result of a dispute over the Government's policy towards manpower cuts in the ground forces. The historian must resist the temptation to stray into the realm of current events, but he may be entitled to ask: are we about to witness the beginning of yet another round of conflict between the French military and the political? History, as I think Mark Twain once remarked, does not often repeat itself, but it does sometimes rhyme, and the rhymes here may have a certain familiarity.

One of the supreme ironies of de Gaulle was that, at the height of the political crisis of 1968, and in a moment of temporary loss of nerve, he should have had to fly to Germany to seek support from Massu, the general he had sacked in Algeria, and canvas the backing of the Army he had broken. But, if the Army at that time had not been an entity aloof from politics, one may well question if de Gaulle's mission would have succeeded. And so the continuing importance of 'specificity' today. In these chapters we have seen the French Army oscillating between various positions; one of them, as identified by a general quoted in Georges Duruy's *L'Officier éducateur*, published in 1904, 'The army is a closed citadel within the nation. It leads its own life because of its special mission, which requires a special education. It has no reason to change.'[52] We also have the conservative General Gallifet, declaring at roughly the same date,[53] 'The Army belongs to no party, it belongs to France,' or again, there is the more strident note, from an admiral justifying the Gaullist coup of 1958, 'At grave hours, when the sovereign voice of the people can no longer express itself, the ARMY suddenly becomes aware of what it is: the People under the Flag. Then, the Army takes responsibility for the People.'[54]

When set against the backdrop of the complexities and responsibilities of modern nuclear warfare, the disobedience of a de Gaulle, or a Weygand, in June 1940 obviously throws up shadows of vast dimensions. The Algerian War showed what can happen when a democratic regime demands too much of the political judgement of its soldiers; with equal clarity it pointed to the need for the military of the West to be taught to think politically in all situations, and to be in touch politically; but not to get involved politically. It is a difficult and dangerous tightrope to have to walk.

In conclusion, as Theodore Zeldin said,

> No nation, no democracy, can write its own history without acknowledging some debt, or some indirect influence to France. French history will always remain of universal historical significance ... France has always had something interesting to say about virtually every aspect of life; I have always found it an unfailing source of stimulation.[55]

I hope that this, perhaps over-ambitious, book will not have persuaded the reader to take a different view.[56]

Notes

Full bibliographical details of works cited below will be found listed in the Sources and Short Reading List.

I Flags in the Wind: The Commune to Dreyfus, 1870–1900

1. Quoted in Ambler, p. 63.
2. Zeldin, II, p. 105.
3. D. Brogan, *France Under the Republic*, p. 700, quoted in Ambler, p. 16.
4. Howard, p. 15.
5. Howard, p. 10.
6. De Gaulle (1932), pp. 10–11; Gorce, p. 191; Ambler, pp. 33, 63.
7. Ambler, pp. 3, 16.
8. Fraser, pp. 36–570.
9. Wavell, p. 20.
10. Bankwitz, p. 212.
11. Secret Session of House of Commons, 10 December 1942; W. S. Churchill, *The Second World War*, vol. IV, p. 575.
12. Georges Laronze, *Histoire de la Commune de 1871; d'après des documents et des souvenirs inédits*, 1928.
13. Horne (1977), p. 353; Maurois, pp. 482, 495.
14. Peyrefitte, p. 255.
15. De Gaulle, p. 67
16. Horne (1965), pp. 59–67.
17. Horne (1965), p. 41.
18. Horne (1965), pp. 40–9.
19. Howard, p. 8.
20. Zeldin, I, p. 508.

21. Tombs, pp. 5–6; Ambler, p. 14.
22. Zeldin, I, pp. 508, 518–19; Paxton, pp. 13–15.
23. In the final plebiscite of 1870, approximately one-sixth of the military were revealed to have voted *No*. (Ralston, p. 16).
24. Tuchman, p. 266.
25. Weber, pp. 74–108, 292–8.
26. Maurois; Zeldin, II, p. 886.
27. Paxton, p. 16; Gorce (2) V, pp. 337–8; Horne (1965), p. 66.
28. Paxton, p. 16; Gorce (2) V, pp. 337–8; Horne (1965), p. 66.
29. P. Paradol, *La France Nouvelle* (1868), p. 276; Horne (1965), p. 63.
30. Ambler, p. 34.
31. Zeldin, II, p. 898; Gorce (2) V, p. 344; Horne (1965), p. 66.
32. Horne (1965), pp. 72–140.
33. Howard, pp. 135, 257–71; Ralston, p. 19; Ambler, p. 15; Horne (1965), p. 140.
34. Bury, p. 86.
35. Horne (1965), *passim.*
36. Tombs, p. 69.
37. Tombs, pp. 33, 125, 144, 197.
38. Tombs, pp. 107–11, 187; Horne (1965).
39. Gorce, p. 27.
40. Zeldin, I, pp. 743–4.
41. Tombs, p. 200.
42. Tombs, p. 63; Bury, p. 146.
43. Horne (1962), pp. 13–14; Horne (1965), p. 509.
44. Weber, pp. 101–8; Ralston, p. 84.
45. Horne (1965), p. 504; Ralston, pp. 46, 62.
46. Howard, p. 455.
47. De Gaulle (1938), from Gorce, p. 6.
48. From Gorce, p. 34.
49. Ralston, pp. 38, 151, 176–200; Porch, pp. 45, 51–2; Gorce, p. 9.
50. Ambler, p. 30; Ralston, pp. 66–76, 137; Porch, p. 14; Gorce, p. 18; Brogan, pp. 127–41; Porch, vii.
51. Brogan, p. 211; King (1), p. 8; Zeldin, I, p. 641; Zeldin, II, p. 898; Maurois, p. 514; Ambler, p. 6; Ralston, pp. 168–173.
52. Paxton, pp. 16–18.

II The Union Sacrée, 1900–18

1. Horne (1962), p. 18; Brogan, pp. 330, 340; Zeldin, I, pp. 679–82; Gorce, pp. 31, 41; Ralston, pp. 213–19.
2. Tuchman, p. 34; Gorce, pp. 45–6; Ralston, pp. 222–6; Brogan, p. 347; Ambler, p. 9.
3. Gorce, p. 46; Horne (1962), p. 18; Bond & Roy, p. 184; Ralston, pp. 220, 232; Porch, p. 61.
4. Gorce, p. 47; Porch, p. 66; Horne (1962), p. 18; Ralston, pp. 243–6.
5. Brogan, pp. 361–6; Horne (1962), p. 18; Zeldin, I, p. 687.
6. Porch, p. 69.
7. Ralston, pp. 261–72; Zeldin, II, pp. 901–2; Gorce, p. 53.
8. Ralston, pp. 261–72; Zeldin, II, pp. 881, 901–2; Gorce, pp. 53–4; Porch, pp. 80, 95–103; Horne (1962), pp. 18–19, 60; Bond & Roy, pp. 124, 129.
9. Porch, pp. 54–5; Ralston, p. 258; Horne (1962), p. 19.
10. Gorce, p. 28.
11. Gorce, pp. 28, 58–61; Ralston, 283–4; King (1), p. 193; Weber, pp. 297–9; Porch, pp. 117–24.
12. Horne (1962), p. 19; Porch, pp. 90, 111, 129; Ralston, p. 284; Gorce, pp. 49–50.
13. Horne (1962), p. 19; Porch, pp. 111, 248–9; Zeldin, II, p. 899; Tuchman, p. 39; Brogan, p. 528; Gorce, p. 56; Bond & Roy, p. 122.
14. Ralston, p. 319.
15. Horne (1962), pp. 19–20; Gorce, pp. 62–96; Ralston, pp. 312–69; Porch, pp. 169–253; Zeldin, I, p. 723; II, pp. 880–3.
16. Horne (1962), pp. 16–17; Maurois, p. 525; Ambler, pp. 11, 46; Porch, pp. 134–68.
17. Horne (1962), pp. 20, 26; Ralston, pp. 239, 315.
18. Brogan, p. 469.
19. Porch, *passim*.
20. Porch, p. 214; Bond & Roy, p. 117.
21. Quoted in Porch, p. 215.
22. Porch, p. 253.
23. Horne (1962), pp. 23–9.
24. Horne (1962), pp. 20, 29–33.
25. Quoted in Ralston, p. 329.
26. Quoted in King (1), p. 28.
27. King (1), p. 14.
28. Quoted in Gorce, p. 105.

29. King (1), p. 47.
30. Brogan, p. 481.
31. Brogan, p. 481.
32. King (1),pp. 47–86; Ralston, pp. 333–7, 374–6; Gorce, pp. 100–15; Zeldin, II, pp. 894–5.
33. King (1), p. 106.
34. King (1), p. 118.
35. Horne (1962), pp. 131–44, 190–1, 313, 326; King (1), pp. 98–142; Gorce, pp. 114–17; Bond & Roy, p. 187; Wavell, p. 24.
36. Quoted in Brogan, pp. 536–7.
37. Quoted in *Oxford Dictionary of Quotations,* pp. 31, 152.
38. Liddell Hart, p. 263.
39. King (1), p. 217.
40. Liddell Hart, p. 331.
41. Quoted in King (1), p. 216.
42. Liddell Hart, p. 323.
43. Gorce, pp. 118–47; King (1), pp. 144–245; Horne (1962), pp. 199, 313–25; Liddell Hart, pp. 254–408; Brogan, pp. 536ff.

III Collapse 1940, 1919–40

1. Horne (1962).
2. Gorce, p. 147.
3. Liddell Hart, pp. 377–81; King (1), p. 220.
4. King (1), pp. 220, 238–40; Liddell Hart, pp. 394–400; King (2), pp. 14–15.
5. As recorded in Foch's posthumous work dictated to Raymond Recouly, *La Memorial de Foch: mes entretiens avec le maréchal* (Paris, 1929).
6. Gorce, p. 148.
7. Quoted in Gorce, p. 170.
8. Quoted in King (2), p. 51.
9. 19 April 1919, quoted in King (2), p. 57.
10. Quoted in King (2), p. 24.
11. Quoted in King (2), p. 26.
12. Quoted in Liddell Hart, p. 422; King (2), p. 132.
13. Gorce, p. 159.
14. Gorce, p. 159.
15. Quoted in Bankwitz, p. 105.

16. Abbé Stephan Coubé, *Alsace, Lorraine et France rhénane; exposé des droits historiques de la France sur toute la rive gauche du Rhin*, quoted in King (2), p. 4.
17. Quoted in King (2), p. 97.
18. Bond & Roy, pp. 187–9; Gorce, pp. 148–80; King (2), pp. v–125; Horne (1969), pp. 37, 42–53; Liddell Hart, pp. 415, 422–4, 431, 438; Zeldin, II, pp. 1092–6.
19. Quoted in Brogan, p. 558.
20. Quoted in Gorce, p. 211.
21. Quoted in Paxton, p. 20.
22. Horne (1969), pp. 42–50, 90, 96; Brogan, pp. 556–8; Tombs, p. 9; Gorce, p. 211; Paxton, p. 20.
23. Quoted in Zeldin, II, p. 896.
24. Gorce, pp. 142–3, 181, 184–204, 208; Horne (1969), pp. 64, 85; Zeldin, II, pp. 895–6.
25. Quoted in Bankwitz, p. 29.
26. Quoted in Bankwitz, p. 20; Gorce, p. 168.
27. Foch had died the previous year.
28. Bankwitz, pp. 5–9, 12–19, 29, 36–9, 75–6, 83–91; Bond & Roy, p. 191; Horne (1969), pp. 60–2; Paxton, p. 165; Ambler, p. 7; Gorce, p. 168.
29. Horne (1969), pp. 56–7.
30. Horne (1969), pp. 105–6.
31. To the Chamber's Army Commission, in 1935.
32. Quoted in Gorce, p. 273.
33. Horne (1969), p. 106.
34. In *Revue des Deux Mondes*, 15 October 1936, quoted in Alexander (1), p. 10.
35. Bond & Roy, pp. 192–3; Zeldin, II, pp. 900–4; Bankwitz, pp. 41, 140, 378; Horne (1969), pp. 56–62, 101–6; Horne (1962), pp. 330–3; Gorce, pp. 235, 271–82; Paxton, p. 166.
36. Peyrefitte, p. 289.
37. Bankwitz, pp. 251, 279; Gorce, pp. 257, 259, 264.
38. Bankwitz, p. 279.
49. Quoted in Bankwitz, p. 173.
40. Gorce, pp. 220, 224–59; Bankwitz, pp. 83, 168–89, 220–59, 268, 321; Horne (1969), pp. 88–95; Paxton, p. 21; Zeldin, II, p. 1147; Ambler, p. 34.
41. Quoted in Bankwitz, p. 225.
42. Bankwitz, p. 378.
43. Bankwitz, pp. 83, 113, 116, 168, 184, 191, 225, 243, 378; Kelly, p. 18; Paxton, pp. 165–9.

44. *Servir*, vol. II, p. 57, quoted in Alexander (2), intro, p. 5.
45. Horne (1969), p. 151.
46. Quoted in Alexander (2), ch. 3, p. 38.
47. Alexander (2), ch. 2, p. 56.
48. Alexander (2), ch. 1, pp. 6–56; ch. 2, pp. 19, 56; ch. 3, pp. 5–61; Alexander (1), pp. 9–15; Bond & Roy, pp. 191–2; Bankwitz, pp. 77, 115; Paxton, p. 166; Gorce, pp. 276–82, 296–7; Ambler, p. 7; Horne (1969), pp. 97–100, 105–120; Zeldin, II, 1091.
49. Quoted Horne (1969), p. 125.
50. Horne (1969), p. 170.
51. Horne (1969), p. 151.
52. Quoted in Ambler, p. 62.
53. Quoted in Horne (1969), p. 215.
54. Bankwitz, p. 310.
55. Bankwitz, p. 310.
56. Bankwitz, pp. 3, 5.
57. Quoted in Bankwitz, p. 309.
58. Bankwitz, p. 318.
59. Quoted in Ambler, p. 56.
60. Horne (1969), pp. 142–656; Bond & Roy (2), p. 76; Bond & Roy (1), p. 198; Fraser, p. 568; Gorce, pp. 304, 309–11; Zeldin, II, p. 885; Horne (1962), p. 337; Bankwitz, pp. 211, 290, 309–10, 323; Ambler, pp. 58–60.

IV The Savage Wars of Peace, 1945–70

1. Gorce, p. 313
2. Gorce, p. 313; Bond & Roy, pp. 197–8 (Ralston).
3. Dwight D. Eisenhower, *Crusade in Europe* (New York), p. 84.
4. At the war's end, each of the (very few) survivors was given the freedom of the Soviet Union and his own private Yak plane; one of the few recorded instances of Soviet recognition of Allied assistance in the Second World War.
5. Letter of 5 December 1942 (quoted in Paxton, p. 392).
6. Keegan, pp. 302–3; Bankwitz, pp. 335–46; Ambler, p. 82; Paxton, p. viii.
7. Keegan, p. 306.
8. Quoted from Paxton, p. 344.
9. Quoted from Raoul Girardet, *Pouvoir civil et pouvoir militaire*

   en France sous la Quatrième République, 1959 (from Paxton, p. 422).
10. Zeldin, II, pp. 885, 904, 1104, 1120; Gorce, pp. 311, 317, 334–5; Ambler, pp. 81–94; Paxton, pp. viii, 21–164, 170–409, 417, 433; Keegan, p. 306.
11. Paxton, p. 426.
12. Paxton, p. 423.
13. Paxton, p. 424.
14. Ambler, p. 94; Gorce, p. 336; Paxton, pp. 410–13, 418, 420–7.
15. Martin, p. 35.
16. Horne (1977), p. 67.
17. Horne (1977), p. 67; Gorce, p. 376; Martin, pp. 35, 93; Keegan, p. 324.
18. Quoted in Horne (1977), p. 175.
19. Bernard de Castelbajac, *La Gloire et leur salaire*, quoted in Gorce, p. 391.
20. Gorce, p. 391.
21. See p. 40.
22. Quoted in Ambler, p. 109.
23. Quoted in Gorce, p. 400.
24. Quoted in Kelly, pp. 24–5.
25. Quoted in Ambler, p. 115.
26. Kelly, pp. 23–54, 130; Horne (1977), pp. 14, 168, 175; Gorce, pp. 338, 354, 360, 385, 390–1, 400, 465, 468; Ambler, pp. 96–7, 103–9; Bankwitz, pp. 365, 369; Paxton, pp. 427, 431.
27. John Gunther, *Inside Africa* (1955), p. 126.
28. Horne (1977), pp. 98–9.
29. Horne (1977).
30. Horne (1977).
31. Horne (1977).
32. Horne (1977), pp. 68, 159, 167, 281, 287, 375, 442, 460; Kelly, p. 147; Gorce, pp. 399, 404, 506–13, 527–30, 542–5; Fall, *passim*; Gunther, *Inside Africa*, p. 126; Ambler, pp. 136–8, 367; Bankwitz, p. 211.
33. Horne (1977), pp. 165–7.
34. Quoted from Bankwitz, p. 372.
35. Horne (1977), pp. 109, 165, 175, 462; Bankwitz, pp. 372, 430; Gorce, pp. 412–19, 433, 446–7, 478–82, 487; Ambler, pp. 217, 313; Kelly, pp. 161, 257.
36. Quoted in Ambler, p. 149.
37. Kelly, p. 200.

38. Ambler, pp. 149, 230, 264; Horne (1977), p. 207; Kelly, p. 200; Gorce, pp. 482–4.
39. See p. 4; De Gaulle (1932), pp. 10–11; quoted in Gorce, p. 191.
40. Ambler, pp. 149, 283, 326, 387; Horne (1977), pp. 167–8, 267, 416; Gorce, pp. 482–5, 468, 506–13; Hernu, pp. 22–4.
41. Quoted in Paxton, p. 424.
42. Quoted in Ambler, p. 282.
43. Paxton, pp. 426–7.
44. Bankwitz, pp. 211, 314, 362–9; Hernu, pp. 22–4; Paxton, pp. viii, 424, 426–7; Horne (1977), pp. 550–3; Martin, p. 23; Ambler, p. 327.
45. Quoted in Kelly, p. 361.
46. France's nuclear deterrent targeted on potential attackers in the West as in the East, literally 'from all points of the compass'.
47. Kelly, pp. 294, 361–80; Horne (1977), pp. 374, 469; S. Highton, *Franco-American Relations*, p. 29; Paxton, p. viii; Martin, pp. 23, 46–84.
48. Gorce, pp. 549, 551–5; Martin, pp. 93, 287–99, 368; Peyrefitte, pp. 140, 234.
49. Howard, p. 2; Hernu, pp. 41, 58, 116, 162, 164; Bankwitz, p. 84; Martin, pp. 120, 129, 148–53, 337; *The Times*, 2 March 1982.
50. Hernu, p. 115.
51. Martin, pp. 287–337; Hernu, pp. 115–16, 162–4, 173, 207; Horne (1977), pp. 551–3; Ambler, p. 373; Gorce, pp. 555–7; Tuchman, p. 284.
52. Quoted in Paxton, p. 428.
53. Quoted in La Gorce, p. 47.
54. Admiral Ortuli, 'Le General de Gaulle, soldat-écrivain-homme d'état', in *Revue de défense nationale*, XV (April 1959), p. 584, quoted in Bankwitz, p. 367.
55. Zeldin, II, pp. 1155, 1172.
56. Kelly, pp. 364–9; *The Times*, 16 June 1982; *Sunday Times*, 20 June 1982; Paxton, p. 428; Bankwitz, pp. 314, 366; Tuchman, p. 284; Gorce, pp. 546–7; Zeldin, II, pp. 1155, 1172.

Sources and Short Reading List

As the research material which provided me with both the inspiration and the matrix for the Lees Knowles lectures was derived from the trilogy of *The Fall of Paris, The Price of Glory*, and *To Lose a Battle*, together with *A Savage War of Peace*, it would be false modesty not to draw attention to the comprehensive bibliographies contained in each volume. The short list below contains some recently published works, supplementary sources more specifically relevant to the subject, or authors referred to in the text. Among unpublished material, I would particularly mention the doctoral thesis by Martin Alexander, written under the auspices of the Franco-British Council and presented at Oxford in 1982: *Maurice Gamelin and the Defence of France 1935–39*.

ALEXANDER, MARTIN, *La faillite de la mécanisation dans les Armées Françaises et Britanniques entre 1935 et 1940 – une étude comparative, 1978*.

ALEXANDER, MARTIN, *Maurice Gamelin and the Defence of France*, 1982.

AMBLER, J. S., *The French Army in Politics, 1945–1962*, Columbus, 1966.

BANKWITZ, PHILIP C. F., *Maxime Weygand and Civil-Military Relations in Modern France*, Cambridge, Mass., 1967.

BOND, BRIAN AND IAN ROY (eds), *War and Society*, London, 1975.

BROGAN, DENIS, *The Development of Modern France, 1870–1934*, London, 1940.

BURY, P. T., *Gambetta and the National Defence*, London, 1936.

FALL, BERNARD, *Hell in a Very Small Place; the Siege of Dien Bien Phu*, London, 1966.

FRASER, RONALD, *Blood of Spain*, London, 1979.

GAULLE, CHARLES DE, *Le Fil de l'Epée*, Paris, 1932.

——, *Vers l'Armée de Métier*, Paris, 1934.

——, *La France et son Armée*, Paris, 1938.

——, *France and her Army*, London, 1945.

GIRARDET, RAOUL, *Société Militaire de France Contemporaine, 1914–15*, Paris, 1953.

GORCE, P. DE LA, *The French Army*, London, 1963.

——, *Histoire du Second Empire*, Paris, 1896.

HERNU, CHARLES, *Citoyen-Soldat*, Flammarion, Collection 'Le Poing Rose', Paris, 1977.

HORNE, ALISTAIR, *The Price of Glory: Verdun 1916*, London, 1962.

——, *The Fall of Paris, the Siege and the Commune 1870–71*, London, 1965.

——, *To Lose a Battle: France 1940*, London, 1969.

——, *A Savage War of Peace: Algeria 1954–1962*, London, 1977.

HOWARD, MICHAEL, *The Franco-Prussian War*, London, 1961.

KEEGAN, JOHN, *Six Armies in Normandy*, London, 1982.

KELLY, GEORGE ARMSTRONG, *Lost Soldiers: the French Army and Empire in Crisis*, Cambridge, Mass., 1947–62.

KING, JERE CLEMENS, *Generals and Politicians: Conflict between France's High Command, Parliament and Government 1914–18*, Univ. of California Press, Berkeley, 1951.

——, *Foch versus Clemenceau: France and German Dismemberment 1918–1919*, Harvard, 1980.

LIDDELL-HART, B. H., *Foch, Man of Orleans*, London, 1931.

MARICHY, JEAN-PIERRE *Le Système Militaire Français*, Toulouse, 1977.

MARTIN, MICHEL LOUIS, *Warriors to Managers: the French Military Establishment since 1945*, Chapel Hill, 1981.

MAUROIS, A, *Histoire de la France*, Paris, 1947.

MENARD, ORVILLE D., *The Army and the Fifth Republic*, Lincoln, Nebraska, 1967.

PAXTON, R. O., *Parades and Politics at Vichy: the French Officer Corps under Marshal Pétain*, Princeton, 1966.

PEYREFITTE, ALAIN, *The Trouble with France*, New York, 1981.

PICKLES, D., *The Fourth Republic*, London, 1958.

——, *The Fifth Republic: institutions and politics*, London, 1962.

PORCH, DOUGLAS, *The March to the Marne*, London, 1981.

RALSTON, DAVID B., *The Army of the Republic: the Place of the*

Military in the Political Evolution of France, 1871–1914, London, 1967.

TOMBS, ROBERT, *The War against Paris*, Cambridge, 1981.

TOURNOUX, JEAN-RAYMOND, *Pétain et de Gaulle*, Plon, Paris, 1964.

TUCHMAN, BARBARA, *Practicing History*, New York, 1981.

WATT, D. C., *Too Serious a Business*, London, 1975.

WAVELL, GENERAL, 'Generals and Generalship', *The Times*, February 1941.

WEBER, EUGENE, *Peasants into Frenchmen, the Modernization of Rural France*, London, 1977.

ZELDIN, THEODORE, *France 1848–1945*, Vols I & II, Oxford, 1973–7.

Index